Carried

HOW ONE MOTHER'S

Trust in God

HELPED HER

THROUGH THE

Unthinkable

Carried

MICHELLE SCHMIDT & ANGIE TAYLOR

DESERET BOOK

SALT LAKE CITY, UTAH

All images courtesy of the Schmidt family except as noted below.
Page 27: Multnomah Falls by Wollertz/shutterstock.com
Page 55: shanecotee/istock/Getty Images
Pages 62 and 124: Busath Photography
Page 104: Courtesy of The Piano Guys
Page 107: Bartfett/istock/Getty Images
Page 163: Photo by Tessa Barton
Page 165: Zach Frank/shutterstock.com
Background: Titus and Co/shutterstock.com

Library of Congress Cataloging-in-Publication Data
Names: Schmidt, Michelle (Michelle Anderegg), author. | Taylor, Angie, 1977– author.
Title: Carried : how one mother's trust in God helped her through the unthinkable / Michelle Schmidt and Angie Taylor.
Description: Salt Lake City, Utah : Deseret Book, [2018] | Includes bibliographical references.
Identifiers: LCCN 2018018737 | ISBN 9781629724782 (paperbound)
Subjects: LCSH: Schmidt, Annie, 1994-2016. | Trust in God. | Bereavement—Religious aspects—The Church of Jesus Christ of Latter-day Saints. | Bereavement—Religious aspects—Mormon Church.
Classification: LCC BX8643.D4 S36 2018 | DDC 248.8/66092—dc23
LC record available at https://lccn.loc.gov/2018018737

Printed in the United States of America
LSC Communications, Harrisonburg, VA

10 9 8 7 6 5 4 3 2 1

Contents

Contents

PART 4: Tributes

Introduction

This story of how my faith carried me and allowed me to navigate a myriad of difficult times in my life could be the story of any girl, young woman, mother, or wife. We all have struggles and hardships that have brought us to our knees. We also all have moments of laughter and great joy. But my story, which includes the tragedy of losing my daughter Annie, became more public due to the nature of my husband's career as a member of The Piano Guys. Because of that publicity, I was the recipient of an outpouring of support and love that was a treasured gift to me and my family.

I wish that each one of you might feel this supported and comforted in the burdens that you carry. It is my hope that my journey of being tutored by God to trust Him more—not only through the loss of Annie but through some of my most vulnerable and personal past experiences—will be the means of bringing strength and hope to anyone suffering at this time. Writing my experience has provided strength and hope for me as well as much-needed healing.

It is also my hope and prayer that my story will help us more fully turn to the giver of every good gift and the source of all love: our Lord and Savior, Jesus Christ. For He carries us through it all and will truly right every wrong, bind up the brokenhearted, comfort those who stand in need of comfort, and ultimately lift us up. "He giveth power to the faint; and to them that have no might he increaseth strength. . . . They that wait upon the Lord shall renew their strength; they shall mount up with wings as eagles; they shall run, and not be weary; and they shall walk, and not faint" (Isaiah 40:29, 31).

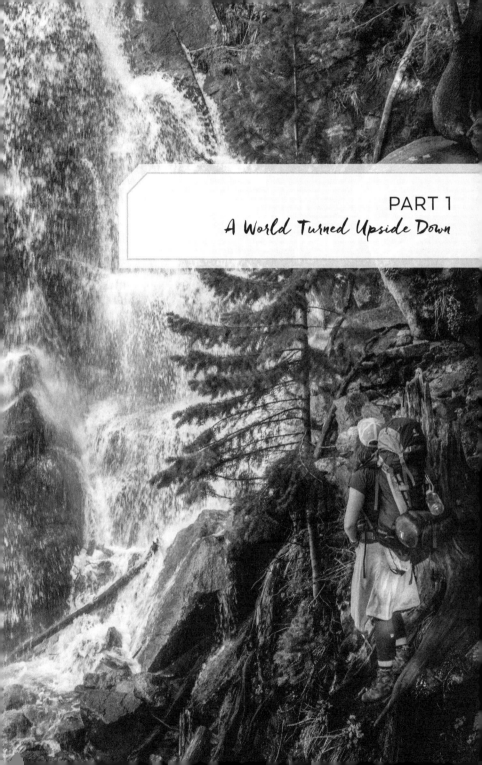

PART 1
A World Turned Upside Down

CHAPTER 1

A Daughter Disappears

Wednesday, October 19, 2016

As the plane made its final descent into Portland, I looked out the window, anxious for my first glimpse of the city Annie loved so much. But thick rain clouds hid what lay beneath, and the plane was soon engulfed in white puffs as it descended through the cloud cover, giving me a slightly uncomfortable feeling when I couldn't see beyond the wing.

Though I was in a large piece of metal racing toward the earth, I focused on the rain streaming across the window in jagged rivulets, each stream careening backward in different paths.

As we exited the clouds and readied for landing, city streets and buildings grew up out of the ground. But just as suddenly as the city appeared, it disappeared among fields of shorn grass whose deep green blades, heavy and engorged with rain, nestled up to the runway.

The edge of the airfield was surrounded by thick pine trees with shrubs and bushes bunched up at their base, making the airport feel secluded from any other life. No one would know that a large, compact city lay just hundreds of yards away. The deep green and all the trees were evidence of why Annie loved this place so much.

Exploring nature filled Annie with joy.

As I exited the airplane and made my way up the ramp to the gate, I called Annie's cell phone, anxious to hear her voice. But the call went straight to voicemail.

"My plane just landed," I said. "Are you here to pick me up?"

I waited before hanging up, absently thinking that if I gave her some time, she would respond to my message any second. But I didn't hear her voice, only the empty silence on the other end. I sent a text instead of calling again, as it was more likely Annie would respond to a text message than a phone call anyway.

I had talked with Annie four days ago, and we had made plans then for her to pick me up at the airport. But I hadn't spoken with her since. Yesterday, I had sent four texts reminding her that I was coming in today. But she didn't respond to any of them, either.

Perhaps her phone was acting up again. It had been on the fritz with battery problems for a while. Fixing her phone was one of the things we needed to do while I was in town.

As I made my way to baggage claim, I admitted the possibility that Annie had completely forgotten I was coming in today, even after all the reminders I'd sent her. She had a tendency to forget important things like this. Maybe she had become distracted with the new camping gear I'd just bought her—the gear we were supposed to use for our camping trip—and had taken it out to test, finding a place she wanted to show me. If she was camping, then her cell battery was probably dead.

I would call and text a few more times, and if she wasn't waiting for me at baggage claim, then I'd rent a car and head to her apartment. Though I felt a slight sense of uneasiness at trying to manufacture reasons why Annie would forget I was coming to town today—she had been so excited about our trip—I prided myself on being levelheaded and sensible. I was sure there was a logical explanation for why she wasn't at the airport.

Once I was settled in a rental car, I Googled directions to her apartment. I soon found out it was nearly impossible to navigate all of the one-way streets in Portland. Which ones would lead me to Annie's apartment quickly and safely? I eventually figured it out, parked, and made my way to the door. After a hurried knock and a short pause, Annie's roommate answered.

"Is Annie here?" I asked.

Annie's roommate stared at me for a couple of seconds before saying in a rush, "I thought she was camping with you." Her surprise and distress at seeing me was evident. "I haven't seen her since Sunday morning." She wrung her hands and shook her head in small back-and-forth movements, as though unsure of what else to say.

"It's okay." I tried to calm her. "There has to be an explanation. Can I come in, and we'll see if we can figure out where Annie is? Maybe she'll show up while I'm here."

But as we sat in the cramped apartment, each silently wondering where Annie could be, I began to seriously worry. It was not like Annie to be gone this long without telling her roommate or someone else where she was going. And now that I thought about it, it was even less like her to not be posting pictures and snaps. I hadn't really realized it until now, but I hadn't seen anything on social media from her for a few days. That was unusual.

"I think I'll look at her online banking," I spoke my thoughts out loud. "Maybe I can track her down by seeing when she made her last purchase."

But scrolling through Annie's online banking activity didn't tell me where she was. She hadn't purchased anything or bought any food since Sunday, at least not with her credit card, which she used for everything.

My stomach began to ache with more anxiety. Something was truly wrong. I needed to do something about it now.

"I'm going to the police station. Hopefully they'll be able to help us find Annie," I announced.

As I made my way back to my car in the dark and rain, which had begun to fall again, I wondered how I was going to find anything in this unfamiliar city. I began to drive, but my rising panic made my thoughts muddled and confused. I was disoriented and couldn't follow the directions on my GPS, and I struggled to navigate the one-way streets at night. Not knowing where to go or what else to do, I pulled into an empty parking lot in an industrial area and called my husband, Jon.

"What if Annie is really missing?" I said. "What are we going to do?" Shock rocked through me as I processed the reality of the situation. I couldn't help imagining all of the horrible things that could have happened to our daughter. But hearing Jon's voice helped me stay focused, and I didn't cry or fall apart. I made myself stay in a "do what needs to be done" mode. Nothing would be accomplished if I lost it.

I got off the phone with Jon and focused on finding a way to the police station. Eventually I found a run-down parking terrace that seemed to be close. I parked and made my way toward a cement stairwell that led out to a rainy street below. I hoped it would get me to the police station.

"Heavenly Father," I said, praying to stay calm while walking around an unfamiliar big city at night by myself, "please help me to get to the police station safely." I imagined being attacked by someone sinister at any moment.

Feeling alone and scared, I called Jon again. He stayed on the phone with me this time while I searched for the police station. It was comforting having him with me even though he was hundreds of miles away. We felt helpless being so far apart from one another.

As I walked toward the station, big windows outside the building, almost like display cases, had pictures of missing persons and persons of interest in local cases. A surge of fear ran through my body as I walked past these to the front doors of the building. Was this really happening to me? Would my daughter's picture be one of those displayed in this window tomorrow? No. My situation would be different. There was a totally reasonable answer as to where Annie was. We just needed to figure it out.

Once inside the building, I made my way to one of the windows, which looked like a movie-ticket booth, and began telling the two men behind the window that my daughter was missing.

It was now nine o'clock at night, and I immediately felt like I had to convince the night-shift crew that I wasn't overreacting, that my daughter really was missing, and that things wouldn't just work themselves out in the morning. If it had been the middle of the day, would the officers have taken me more seriously?

"Just take a seat over there, and someone will be out to help you," one of the officers said, pointing to some chairs behind me.

I sat down and waited, unable to stop myself from imagining the worst.

When an officer came out, he riddled me with questions that again made me feel as if I had to convince him that I wasn't overreacting. "Was your daughter suicidal? Has she been using drugs? Did the two of you have an argument recently?"

My anxiety only increased, as I knew this line of thinking wasn't going to lead us to Annie.

"Ask the officer if it's okay if you say a prayer with him," Jon said over the phone, helping in the best way he knew how.

I felt particularly awkward asking the officer if we could pray. But Jon and I had made a goal to try to involve Heavenly Father in all our doings, and we desperately needed His help.

"Do you mind if we say a prayer?" I asked.

The officer looked uncomfortable but nodded.

"Father in Heaven," I said, and then I began to cry. I was suddenly unable to maintain my walls of strength; they all came tumbling down as I bowed my head and reached out to God for the first time out loud since discovering Annie's absence. "Please help us to find Annie. Please help this officer and anyone else who will work with him. Please bless them to work to the best of their abilities to help us find our daughter."

As I finished my prayer, I noticed a definite softening and gentleness in the way the officer treated me. "I'll get an officer on the case right away," he said. "We will contact you as soon as we can."

I left the station and began searching for a place to stay for the night. I didn't want to go back to Annie's apartment. It was too small, and I needed to be alone so I could process my emotions.

I drove around downtown Portland looking for a hotel and eventually found a place that had an available room. It was almost midnight, and I was exhausted and needed to get some rest so that I could figure out what I was going to do next.

And so began the worst night of my life.

Waiting to hear from the officer, waiting for any of this to make sense, I crawled into bed still in my clothes, shivering, and began to discuss on the phone with Jon every scenario of where Annie might be. Every possible outcome we came up with was horrifying. Realistically considering the many possibilities of what could have happened to Annie—having been kidnapped, forced into sex trafficking, or that her body, at this very moment, was experiencing abuse and torture and eventual murder—was the worst mental hell I had ever experienced.

"But maybe none of these things have happened," Jon said. "Maybe Annie went hiking and is lost and injured, just waiting for someone to find her." Though the worst-case scenarios were hard to ignore, Jon's words made me cling to hope.

The officer eventually called, and we began a three-way conference call with the officer launching into asking all kinds of questions.

"As important as these questions might seem," Jon said adamantly, "the most important thing we should do is to get a ping from Annie's phone of her last location. That is the only way we are even going to know where to start."

"That can't be authorized because your daughter is over eighteen," the officer said matter-of-factly. "Unless we have certain proof that Annie is in danger of committing suicide, we have to wait for a warrant to invade her privacy. That could take a few days." The officer stated these facts as if reciting memorized information.

"But we are Annie's parents. Are you saying we have to wait three or four more days to have the authority to ping her phone, which might take us straight to her?" Jon's voice was calm but it rang with frustration. "In the meantime, are we just supposed to hope that Annie isn't being raped or molested, or isn't injured on a mountain somewhere suffering in the rain, hoping and praying that someone will find her, all because of some ridiculous protocol?" Jon was furious at this point.

The officer reaffirmed what we could legally do for the time being, and Jon and he continued their heated argument. It was extremely painful to know we might have located Annie sooner rather than later if we didn't have to worry about a ludicrous law that took away our parental rights to find her and bring her safely home.

When we ended the call with the officer, Jon said he would look for Annie by calling everyone and everywhere he could, beginning with contacting the hospitals in the area. "Either way, I'll fly in tomorrow with Spencer, and we'll begin searching," he said. I was anxious for his arrival with Spencer, our oldest son, knowing that I wouldn't have to face this by myself.

We said one last prayer together before hanging up, and then I tried to get some sleep.

But as I lay there, falling in and out of consciousness, pleading with Heavenly Father for my Annie to be protected, to be safe until we found her, my personal hell consumed my thoughts, bringing the worst possibilities concerning Annie's whereabouts into my mind.

As I thought of what some disgustingly malevolent person could be doing to Annie's body, I pled and pled with God.

"Please, Father! Please keep Annie safe. Anything but forced sex and murder. Please! I've made covenants with Thee in the temple." I called upon the priesthood power I had been endowed with in the temple, knowing it could bless me and my children. "Please keep Annie safe. Please help us find her. Please! Please! Please!"

I pled and wrestled all night, crying out to the Lord in exhaustion. It was hell. Unbearable, painful, horrible.

CHAPTER 2

Hearing the Voice of God

I was raised by a strong family in the gospel of Jesus Christ, restored through the Prophet Joseph Smith. My parents had strong testimonies of Heavenly Father and of our Savior, Jesus Christ. Though my family was less than perfect, there were wonderful and amazing qualities I gained from my parents. One of those qualities was faith and an ability to hear the voice of God.

I was the first of my parents' seven children. At birth I appeared to be perfectly healthy, but as the months went on, I began throwing up about every fourth meal. At first, this didn't seem too out of the ordinary. But as time passed, it began to feel unusual, even suspicious. When I was about six months old, my parents took me to the doctor to have my stomach checked. The doctor couldn't detect any visible abnormalities, so he ordered X-rays to see if there was anything else going on that he couldn't see from the outside.

After the X-rays were taken and the radiologist and doctor had analyzed them, the doctor said he would like to take some more pictures, but this time of my back. My mom wondered, "What does her back have to do with her throwing up?"

After viewing both the stomach and back X-rays, the doctor explained that the stomach X-rays showed no signs whatsoever of any abnormalities, but that the back X-rays detected major deformities of the vertebrae and spinal cord. At the time, the doctor was not very familiar with the extent of the malformations, and he strongly suggested that my parents find a specialist.

Finding a specialist proved to be a hard undertaking, because every doctor my parents went to in Salt Lake said, "I feel unqualified to handle this situation." As the months went on, my parents, and especially my mom's parents, Grandma and Grandpa Pearce, were determined to find a doctor who could not only diagnose my birth defect but also propose a course of action.

As I think about my parents going through this with their first child, I see how their faith was stretched and strengthened through their struggling and pleading with the Lord for me. During this time, I stopped throwing up. In fact, I hadn't thrown up since the X-rays that led doctors to discover the birth defect. This was a testimony to my parents that the Lord had His hand in leading them to discover the abnormality through miraculous means, and that He would continue to help them as they sought a doctor.

My Grandpa Pearce was determined, and he finally found

a doctor at the Mayo Clinic in Rochester, Minnesota, who would take our case. The doctor was a young Catholic man named Dr. MacCarthy who specialized in spinal cord issues. He diagnosed my defect as diastemetamymelia: a bifurcation or splitting of the spinal cord in a small area, in addition to deformed vertebrae. Diastemetamymelia had existed before my 1967 case. But because there were no outward signs of malformations, it had never been discovered until the spinal cord would break or tear, and the person became paralyzed.

Dr. MacCarthy was willing to do a first-time-ever surgery on me to try to wrap something around the spinal cord to put it back together. The outcome of this surgery was completely unknown, and it couldn't be determined whether touching the spinal cord, no matter how delicately, would result in paralysis. Again, my parents' faith was stretched as they prayed to know if they should risk doing the surgery.

Through marriage we were related to Gordon B. Hinckley, who at the time was a member of the Quorum of the Twelve Apostles and who would later be sustained as President of The Church of Jesus Christ of Latter-day Saints. My parents went to him seeking a blessing for me, and Elder Hinckley gave a blessing of power and assurance that the operation would be successful.

In my mother's own words, which she recorded and put in my scrapbook in 1968, she wrote:

In August, 1967, when she was nine months old, Michelle Anderegg was anointed with oil by her father, Jerry Anderegg, and given a blessing for the sick in the household of faith by apostle and friend, Gordon B. Hinckley. He prayed as one having authority and expressed the following ideas: He blessed Michelle that through the power of the holy Melchizedek Priesthood she would be able to withstand the operation. Not only would she be able to withstand the operation, but he blessed her to be entirely whole of body. He blessed her physicians "to perform with skill beyond their normal capacities." Dr. MacCarthy, who was the head neurosurgeon, later described his part in the operation using nearly the exact wording used in the blessing. The doctor also added, "I felt as if the Lord had his arm around me the entire time."

Elder Hinckley went on forcefully to rebuke the destroyer, that he wouldn't have power over Michelle. He blessed that she would have a bright future and be able to run and walk freely. He blessed her mother and father and loved ones that they would have faith and pray always and know of the power of the priesthood. This blessing was a witness to that truthfulness of the gospel and to the holy power of the priesthood.

My mom and dad, Cathy and Jerry Anderegg; Grandpa Pearce; and me.

For after a five-hour operation, with many blood transfusions, Michelle, within a short period of time of entering the recovery room, began to crawl, demonstrating that no damage had incurred during the surgery to the spinal cord. Since that wonderful recovery and prophetic blessing, Michelle has lived a healthy, normal life.

It is my prayer that she will use her healthy body in service to the Lord, who obviously needs her to perform a great work here on earth. For we were led to find the defect in a truly miraculous manner. . . . This is my record and testimony, in the name of Jesus Christ, Amen.

Cathy Anderegg

I'm not sure I'm meant to do "a great work." But I do know that all of our lives are "a great work" if we seek to fulfill the Lord's purposes.

After this surgery, I was blessed to grow up living a mostly normal life. Though my back was weak, I was able to do most things. Hiking, especially backpacking, and walking or standing for long periods of time were always really hard on my back, but I learned to live with the weakness and bouts of pain, and I was determined to not let them slow me down much.

In high school I wanted to be a cheerleader more than anything. My parents, especially my dad, were opposed to it, since our cheer squads were competitive and did all kinds of routines with stunts, tumbling, and building human pyramids. As you can imagine, my parents were concerned that this would be too dangerous for my back. But I didn't care one bit. I was going to die if I wasn't a cheerleader. So I went ahead and tried out, and I made it. And just like my parents had worried it would, cheerleading proved to be extremely hard on my back, making it ache all the time. Again, I didn't care. I was willing to go to any limits to be a part of the team.

At a summer practice in 1984, we decided as a team that we were going to build a four-man-high human pyramid. We were accustomed to building three-man pyramids, and we were well known among the other schools for doing some of the hardest and most dangerous pyramids and stunts. I took great pride in this.

On an early June morning, before our adviser arrived at our practice, we began trying to build this four-man pyramid, which I was to be the top of. We tried a few times, one layer at a time, and each time people couldn't hold it, and we fell down. And each time, as I fell from three people high to the ground, I felt a zing of pain go up my spine, as though the Holy Ghost were warning me to stop. But, completely disregarding the warnings of the Spirit, I persisted in trying to stick this pyramid. Finally, on our last attempt to build the pyramid, as the pyramid came tumbling down, my right foot landed on someone else's foot, and it broke my foot off inward. The break was a compound dislocated fracture that left my foot hanging to the side of my leg. Not only did this injury put a stop to all dangerous cheerleading activities, it put an end to many physical activities for the rest of my life. Though the ramifications of this foot injury were hard to accept, it did protect my back throughout my life.

These physical struggles, especially those with my back, were just a part of life as I knew it, and I learned to take them in stride. I think they might have given me an ever-present sense that I was so blessed to be able to walk, and that this was a miraculous gift given to me from a loving Heavenly Father. This truth is something I've carried with me always.

My faith in hearing the voice of God was also strengthened shortly after I was baptized and received a Book of Mormon, which I tried to read from every day. At the time, I didn't understand much of what I read. But what I did understand scared me.

I understood that there were two groups of people who always fought with each other, and that there were prophecies about similar wars and rumors of wars in the latter days. I prayed earnestly at night for protection from these impending wars. As the intensity of my prayers increased, the intensity of my sincerity and heartfelt emotion increased.

During this time as a young child, reading my scriptures and saying my prayers, I thanked Heavenly Father for my many blessings. I had the idea that I needed to show emphasis for my gratitude by saying "thank you" a number of times for each subject. For example, I would begin with things I was less thankful for, and they would get only one or two thank-yous. "Thank you for this day. Thank you for the sun." And then, "Thank you, thank you for our food. Thank you, thank you for our house." And then, "Thank you, thank you, thank you for my mom. Thank you, thank you, thank you for my dad," and so on.

I went on counting my thank-yous for a number of months, feeling like I needed to count them up to show how grateful I was. Sometimes these prayers became kind of complicated as I lost track of how many thank-yous I had said, and I'd have to go back to the beginning and say them again.

In my childlike mind, it never occurred to me that this

way of praying was not necessary. But these prayers were offered in absolute sincerity as I felt such a strong desire to express my gratitude.

One night, I finished reading my scriptures and turned off my lights and knelt next to my bed to say my prayers. I can still picture the darkness of my room and the light that glowed under the foot of my door from the hallway on the other side. I began my prayer, praying for protection and safety. And then I began my prayers of gratitude by counting my thank-yous.

Suddenly, and completely unexpectedly, I heard a voice that spoke clearly to my mind and heart. "You do not need to count your thank-yous. I can feel how grateful you are."

Feeling a little scared, I jumped into my bed and got under my covers. There I sat quietly and tried to comprehend what had happened. A feeling of love surged through me and filled me with overwhelming peace. I looked around my room in total shock.

Had I just heard a voice? I mean, had I really heard a voice speak to me in my room? Yes. I had. And it had come from Heavenly Father. He was real! I had always believed He was real. Of course, I had believed in Him. That was why I was praying to Him and speaking with Him. But this experience made Him more real. He was really listening to me.

And I thought, "He talked to me. He loves me. He knows how thankful I am. He's heard all of my prayers. He hears everybody's prayers!"

This knowledge of the reality of God, the Eternal Father, gained at such a young age, has been with me ever since. And because of that knowledge, I've talked to God throughout my life. I've talked to Him when I've been sad. I've talked to Him when I've needed to repent. I've talked to Him when I've been scared. I've asked Him to guide me, direct me, correct me, forgive me, show me, and save me. He has become an integral part of my life. He *is* real, and He hears our prayers.

However, since that childlike prayer all those years ago, there have been many times I've wondered why He doesn't always talk with me like He did then. If He could speak audibly to me then, why didn't He always speak clearly and give me direction and answers like I knew He was capable of doing?

Even as I've asked this question, I've instinctively known the answer: this life is mine to struggle through; it is my task to learn to seek and wrestle for answers. How will my faith ever grow if I have everything handed to me? For Him to do so would undermine my spiritual progress.

And yet, when Annie went missing, I wanted definite interactions from the spirit world, interactions like I've never wanted before. I wanted tangible answers and feelings of consolation. I yearned for spiritual knowledge like I've never experienced before. I knew Heavenly Father was hearing my prayers, but never before had the veil felt so thick and so definite. Why was He being so silent?

Then one day, I thought about my innocent, childlike experience of hearing my Heavenly Father's voice, and the thought came to me, "What were you doing when He spoke to you then?"

"What was I doing?" I asked myself. "I was praying."

"No. *How* were you praying?"

And the answer came: I was expressing my gratitude.

"Not only were you expressing gratitude, you were consumed with the desire that Heavenly Father would feel and know and understand how grateful you were. You wanted Him to truly know how much you appreciated Him. You expressed, to the best of your ability, your complete, utter, and all-consuming love. How could He help but reach back to you and tell you He loved you too?"

Realizing this, I asked myself, "When was the last time I was so filled with a desire of showing my gratitude and love that Heavenly Father knew and felt how grateful I was?" It had not been nearly enough recently.

The scriptures say, "And he who receiveth all things with thankfulness shall be made glorious; and the things of this earth shall be added unto him, even an hundred fold, yea, more" (Doctrine and Covenants 78:19).

Since this continued realization, I've tried more and more to express my gratitude for my blessings and for the many times I've heard God's voice and seen His hand in my life. At times, expressing my gratitude has been extremely difficult because all I can think about is how much I need help and how worried I am about things. Because of that, I've had to work extra hard to become a more grateful person. And I've come to believe that if I truly want to rend the veil and hear God's voice more, I need to grow in appreciation for Him. I need to grow in my understanding of Him. As I've sought to do so, I've felt my closeness to Him grow stronger and stronger.

CHAPTER 3

Hearing Annie's Voice

Thursday, October 20, 2016–Friday, October 21, 2016

The next day, I woke weary and with a heavy soul. The rain that fell outside in a huge deluge, turning the streets into rivers, brought the locals outside with their phones to film the overflowing spectacle.

"Is Annie stranded somewhere in this storm, trying to survive the cold? Is her body holding onto life, shaking fiercely?" I wondered.

Trying not to become consumed by these thoughts, which were debilitating, I worked tirelessly all day to hack into Annie's Twitter, Instagram, Snapchat, and Facebook accounts, sending out message after message, asking if anyone knew where she was.

Meanwhile, I received a call from the detective who was assigned to Annie's case, gathering as much information as she could:

"What was Annie wearing when you last saw her? How was she acting? What kind of a mood was she in? Is there anything missing from the apartment? Did she take her camping gear with her? What shoes was she wearing when she left? What kind of books was she reading? How was her emotional state in the last month?"

The detective's questions ran on, and I began to feel more frustrated than ever that we seemed to be getting nowhere.

Finally, permission was granted to have Verizon locate a ping on Annie's phone. I thought, "Yes! Now we'll get somewhere." But Verizon didn't get back to us for what felt like forever. I couldn't understand it. I kept thinking, "Isn't locating a ping on a cell phone an easy thing to do?" But in this case, it wasn't, which was extremely frustrating and added to the fact that finding Annie depended on so many variables, and an entire day was slipping away in the pouring, gushing rain, without giving us any leads.

However, in the late afternoon, I received a phone call from the Hood police station. They had found Annie's car parked on an off-ramp of Highway 40 near the Tooth Rock Trailhead in the Columbia River Gorge National Forest. Evidence showed that the car had been there for a while, as the windows were broken out and the radio was gone. But other than that, there was no reason to suspect foul play.

This was amazingly comforting information to me. It supported the probability that Annie had gone hiking and had gotten lost or injured, which made total sense to me, since she went hiking by herself all the time.

Later that evening, we received word from Verizon that Annie's last ping had come from inside her car. This made the police assume that she must have left her phone in her car, and it had been stolen along with the radio when someone broke into the vehicle.

But this didn't make any sense to me. Why would Annie go hiking without taking her phone? She always took it with her on hikes to capture pictures of beautiful waterfalls or amazing scenic views from the edge of a cliff. I considered the possibility that her phone had been acting up again and that the battery hadn't been functioning correctly, so it was possible she had left it behind. Regardless, there was no sign of where her phone was now.

Overall, Thursday ended up being an excruciating day of trying to get information from the cell-phone company, the police department, and the missing persons detective; of Jon and Spencer arriving in Oregon; of talking with family, local Church leaders, and search and rescue teams; and of reaching out to anyone and everyone on every social media avenue we could think of who might know where Annie was—a whole day gone with the rain pouring mercilessly down.

Friday morning dawned clear, which meant we were able to begin the official search for Annie. But as I awoke, and the reality of what my day held descended upon me, dread washed over me. How could I face the day? How could I even get out of bed? I felt as though I didn't have the ability to do so.

Suddenly the words from a hymn came into my mind: "Bruised, broken, torn for us on Calvary's hill" ("Jesus of Nazareth, Savior and King," *Hymns* [1985], no. 181). And I knew that because Christ had been bruised, broken, and torn on a hill, because He had already done this for us, He would be able to help Annie in whatever situation she was in. *He* had already suffered whatever *she* was experiencing on *her* hill.

Then more words came into my mind, "Life evermore we'll know through thee, our Friend." And the feeling filled my soul that, no matter what Annie's current circumstances were, she would be saved and live again through Jesus Christ, our Friend. These truths gave me the strength to get up and out of bed.

The strength I received would soon be tested, as the day started off with our rental car being locked in a parking garage. We couldn't get it out until 9:00 a.m., and the search was to begin at 7:00 a.m. The situation tested my patience. But I tried to stay calm and figure out what to do next while I waited to get the car out. In the meantime, Jon and Spencer were able to get a ride with someone else up to the search and rescue base camp.

As I waited in the dark morning for the parking garage to open so I could get the rental car out, I kept thinking, "Is this really happening? Is this real life? I feel like I'm in a movie." And I honestly did feel as though I were in a movie, moving about as if I were fully present and yet feeling only half conscious. Even now it's impossible to explain how I felt while sitting in the hotel eating area with the local morning news showing Annie's picture, and reporters asking if anyone had any news regarding her whereabouts, and to please report it to the local authorities if they did.

Again, I thought, "Is this really happening? Does anyone in this room know that the story on the TV is about my daughter? Is anyone even listening? Does it even matter to them? *My* whole world is turned inside out. *My* life will never be the same. Can this be real?"

Later, when I was finally able to get the rental car and

begin the drive up to the search and rescue site, I had a moment alone to reflect. As I turned off the main highway and began the drive east up Highway 40 along the Columbia River, I noticed the breathtaking beauty surrounding me.

It was a crisp fall morning, and the sky was clear and crystal blue after the storms of the previous day. And though the sky was clear, a mist and a scattering of intermittent clouds dotted the mountains to the right of the gorge. The colors were the most vibrant greens and blues I had ever seen. The river to my left was striking, lined on either side with gorgeous deep green trees. And the mountains to my right were stunning, with waterfalls, moss-covered mountainsides, and huge trees that overwhelmed my ability to take it all in. Even now, I'm completely unable to describe with mere words the beauty of the Columbia River Gorge.

Multnomah Falls.

When the reality of what I was seeing overcame me, and I felt a deep spiritual awe at the overwhelming beauty, I spontaneously said, "Oh, Annie! I get it. I'm blown away at how beautiful this place is. No wonder you love it so much. No wonder you wanted me to see this so badly."

And, as unexpectedly as I spoke to her, she spoke back, saying, "I know, Mom. I told you it was so beautiful! I'm so happy you are able to see this and to love it the way I do."

I held very still, realizing I had experienced a moment that would take me a minute to understand, just like when I was a little girl saying my "thank-you" prayers and heard Heavenly Father speak to me. I thought to myself, "I just heard and felt Annie speak to me. It was every bit my Annie. She was so excited and animated and responded exactly how Annie would have if she had been here in real life."

It *was* Annie's voice, and we'd had a perfect conversation. But there was one problem. If I had truly been able to hear Annie's voice, it was because she was in the spirit world, no longer alive on this earth.

And yet, the voice I'd heard, Annie's voice, hadn't seemed alarmed or distressed in any way. She hadn't seemed worried that she had passed on. Instead, she was ecstatic that I was overcome with the beauty around us, just as much as she was. It was a bonding experience, and I felt a deep connection of love between us. Most important, it filled me with a calm peace and assurance that Annie was completely fine. She wasn't suffering or in pain. She was happy.

As a mother facing days and weeks ahead of searching for my missing daughter, days filled with speculation and all kinds of insinuations surrounding her disappearance by so many well-intentioned people, this one short moment with Annie's spirit brought me more comfort and strength and peace than I can possibly describe.

That isn't to say that I didn't feel sick in my stomach any-time someone questioned why we had ruled out "foul play" as the cause of Annie's disappearance. And yes, it was hard when someone would call the police saying they had just seen Annie on a bus heading south in California, or some such thing, as if there still might be a glimmer of hope that she was alive.

Yet, for the most part, my experience of hearing Annie's voice and knowing that she was in the spirit world gave me an inner knowledge and peace that my little girl was completely fine, and that what we were searching for was just her physical body.

Until then, I had never realized how precious that physical body was to me. More than anything, I wanted to find that body and bring it safely home. I wanted the closure that it would bring to be able to bury her body, kind of like tucking a child securely into bed at night.

At one point, I remember reasoning with Heavenly Father, telling Him, "I helped create that body. Do I have any claim to it? Because if I do, will you please lead us to it?"

Ironically, Annie had spent so much time abhorring that body because she was a full-figured girl and hated it with all of her heart. It had been difficult to be the mother of a daughter who was so unhappy with her body. Shopping for everyday clothes or for dresses for dances was always the worst, most agonizing experience. I would say, "Just because being a stick is really popular in high school doesn't mean it's popular in the real world. There are many beautiful women in the world who are full-figured." But, at the time, Annie never seemed to believe me.

I hoped that one day she would believe me and realize that every woman, at some point in her life, has to come to peace with her body. That doesn't mean that we shouldn't stay healthy and try to feel good about ourselves. But when it comes down to it, we need to be happy with the body we have. Some of us don't have any waist and some of us do. Some of us have short legs and some have long. Some of us gain sixty pounds when we get pregnant, others barely show, and some aren't able to become pregnant at all in this life. Some of us have clear skin and some of us don't. Some of us have thick hair and some of us have thin. We can spend our entire lives being unhappy with ourselves, or we can choose to love what we have been given. When we embrace what we have and seek to make the best of it, then we can let go of the constant obsession of being unhappy with ourselves; we can become beautiful, confident women.

I love the peace and self-assurance Annie shows in this picture.

At the time of Annie's death, I believe she was beginning to be happy with herself and with her body and what she looked like. In one of the last pictures taken of her, she is looking up into the sky with her beanie on, and I see a feeling of peace and self-assurance exuding from her eyes.

So, when Annie's spirit left her body, I believe she turned and looked at her body and thought to herself, "That was a great body. Why did I spend so much time being unhappy with it? It served me well. It was strong. It could do crazy hikes. It was such a great, healthy body. I'm thankful for that wonderful, beautiful body of mine."

Therefore, when the first search began and the on-camera interviews ensued, which were so surreal and raw, I was unguarded, vulnerable, unscripted, unable to pretend that I believed Annie was still alive. I was criticized for some of the initial interviews I gave because of it. I understand why that would be upsetting to people. I'm sure I appeared unfeeling as a mother to express a belief that my daughter was dead without showing signs of losing my mind. But the personal witness I had received that we were searching just for Annie's body, and that she was safe and happy in the spirit world, gave me the greatest peace and comfort.

At one point in the day somebody said to me, "I sure hope this has a good outcome." I thought to myself, "It will. The outcome is guaranteed. Christ made sure of that long ago. He has guaranteed our outcome."

CHAPTER 4

The Wisdom in Creating This Earth

"He hath made the earth by his power, he hath established the world by his wisdom, and hath stretched out the heaven by his understanding" (Jeremiah 51:15).

Throughout my life, sometimes I've questioned the wisdom of the creation of this world, especially as I've looked at the suffering some people experience. When I've thought about what a child might be going through at this very moment as a victim of child sex trafficking, for example, I'm filled with pain. As I've ached and shrunk from the evil realities that exist in the world, I've looked to the heavens and said, "Are you sure creating this world was a good idea?"

Seeking comfort from the evil that exists around us, I recently studied all the references to Jesus Christ in the scriptures and found myself studying about Christ as the Creator. As I pondered about God's wisdom in creating this world, my thoughts were very much consumed with the upcoming anniversary of the passing of my Annie. And in thinking about these two all-consuming realities—Christ as Creator and Annie's passing—I realized that the wisdom behind the creation of this world and our existence is for the sole purpose of forming family bonds.

Without my opportunity to come to this earth, I never would have had the opportunity to unite myself to my husband. I would have remained a single intelligence forever. Through marriage, I've had the opportunity to become more than I was singly. I've become "one" with my husband to the degree that my thoughts, emotions, feelings, ideas, and identity have become intertwined with his, truly uniting us.

This unity is synergistic, in that one plus one is greater than two. It equals limitless power and growth and progression. This union is a blessing to the degree that it has changed me to become a completely different and evolved intelligence, more so than I could have experienced on my own. Sharon Eubank, first counselor in the Relief Society General Presidency, defines this union as the "divine pair" ("This Is a Woman's Church," https://www.fairmormon.org/conference/august-2014/womans-church).

The absolute beauty and miracle of the "divine pair" is that we are given authority to become co-creators with Christ. We are given permission and the stewardship to bring more life onto this earth. And these spirits who come to us as our children are absolute little miracles. Since we are bound to them with such strong ties of love and loyalty and commitment, the familial bond between parent and child is beyond mortal understanding.

When I gave birth to my first child, I remember being blown away at how much I loved him. As I held my newborn son, I would sit, ponder, and marvel that I loved someone as much as I loved him. I thought to myself, "Did my parents love me this much? They must have, but I had no idea they loved me this much!" I remember thinking, "I would cut off both arms and legs if it meant it was the only way to save this child. I would take poison. I would become paralyzed for him. I would do absolutely *anything* for him!" And, as a new mother, I worked my hardest to try to do anything and everything possible for my newborn son, who was now under my stewardship.

Thinking back, I was so unrealistic. I thought being a good mother meant doing everything I could for my baby, including staying awake when he was awake and sleeping when he slept. As a result, I didn't get him on a sleep schedule; if he woke up in the middle of the night, I would sit up with him, trying so hard to stay awake and interact with him instead of trying to get him back to sleep. I thought that every one of his waking moments should be spent with me giving him my full attention. (Is it any wonder he still feels like I should be giving him my undivided attention the second he walks into the room?) But I couldn't help myself. I loved my baby boy more than life itself, and I absolutely lost myself, in the best way possible, to motherhood.

Then I became pregnant with a girl. I thought, "A girl? How could I love a girl? Will it feel weird to have a girl? Will I ever love her as much as I love my son?"

For some reason, these crazy thoughts were an underlying fear I experienced throughout my pregnancy with Annie, right up until the moment I first saw her. But when I did, the first thing I said was, "I love her so much. She is so beautiful!"

Then I continued on and on about how beautiful and wonderful she was. I would ask Jon and any nurse who came in the room, "Have you ever seen such a beautifully perfect feminine baby?"

In addition, Annie was such a delight. She was aware and perceptive. She began smiling in her second week. And, no, it was not just gas, because she kept doing it. She couldn't really hold her head up at all, but the second she locked eyes with you, she'd give you a huge smile. Really! And that was exactly what she did all her life: look right into the eyes of whoever was near and try to smile joy from her face right down deep into their heart.

I kept a record of when my children hit different milestones, and it was unbelievable to me how fast Annie did everything. It was as though she were on some kind of accelerated schedule:

Sweet Annie hiding in the red rocks of St. George, Utah.

2 weeks—gave a real smile
3 months—rolled over
4 months—sat up
5 months—first tooth
6 months—moved from sitting to knees, scooting around
7 months—crawled
8 months—pulled herself up, hands in toilet
9 months—walked
10 months—climbed out of crib, won't stay in
12 months—talked

Annie was always on the go. Always climbing and always wanting to squeeze into little tiny spaces.

Looking back, it's funny how much I worried that I wouldn't know how to love a girl as much as I loved my son. It turned out I was able to love a girl just as much as a boy, and the miracle of it was, my love for one in no way diminished my love for the other. It was the same way when each of my five children was born. It was as if my capacity to love just increased, changing me forever.

So, when I've wondered if the creation of this world was worth all the heartache and terror that exists in it, I know that, for me personally, it was. Because the bonds in a family are so strong that they go beyond the grave, they go beyond separation, and misunderstandings, and even abuse.

This means that even though I'm separated physically from Annie right now, she is mine. She is my daughter, and she will be my daughter forever and ever, into the eternities. When I pass from this life to the next, I'll be reunited with her again. That might mean I'll be separated from my other children for a time. But eventually we'll all be together again, and nothing but a preference for evil over good will be able to separate us. And what joy that will be!

I had an experience that gave me an inkling of the kind of joy I'll feel when I'm reunited with Annie, with Jon, and with my other children in the next life.

Right after my son Spencer's two-year mission, we went to Seattle, Washington, as a family to pick him up. We arrived early in the morning at his apartment, and he was such a blast to be reunited with. We all hugged, and he started talking a mile a minute telling us the most hilarious stories, just like old times, as if we hadn't skipped any time or had any moments apart.

Then we got in the car and drove to an IHOP to get breakfast. It was pretty early, so there were no other customers in the restaurant. The hostess seated us in a private back corner of the restaurant at a big, round booth where we all fit in together.

Breakfast at IHOP with Sarah, Chris, Elder Schmidt, Jonny, and Annie.

For a moment, we sat together in silence, with Spencer surrounded by two siblings on either side leaning in on him, hugging him. Then a feeling descended upon us unlike any I've ever experienced, all together as a family, before or since. It was a spirit of love and unity that came upon each one of us so powerfully. All we could do was sit there in silence with tears streaming down our faces, basking in the warmth and love that had overcome us.

If my joy at being reunited with Annie on the other side of the veil is anything like the love and unity our family experienced the day we were reunited with Spencer, then heaven will be enough for me. All the hardships that this life has held, and will hold, will have been worth it.

So, what of the horrors that coexist on this planet with the forming of loving family bonds? What about the inconsistencies in family life, the ironies, the unfairness, and the reality of evil? How are all these hardships worth it? The answer is the Savior, Jesus Christ. He is the only way that this plan works. It is the promise from the Father given to us that "the Son of righteousness [will] arise with healing in his wings" (3 Nephi 25:2). He has the ability to right every wrong, make fair every unfairness, heal every pain and sorrow, and compensate for every loss.

Someday I hope I'll be able to watch Annie fall in love and have a family, and to be there for her when she bears her own children. I trust in this prophetic promise: "The Lord has promised that in the eternities no blessing will be denied His sons and daughters who keep the commandments, are true to their covenants, and desire what is right. Many of the most important deprivations of mortality will be set right in the Millennium, which is the time for fulfilling all that is incomplete in the great plan of happiness for all of our Father's worthy children. We know that will be true of temple ordinances. I believe it will also be true of family relationships and experiences" (Dallin H. Oaks, *With Full Purpose of Heart* [2010], 35).

CHAPTER 5

Search and Rescue

Friday, October 21, 2016–Sunday, October 23, 2016

When I arrived at the base camp for Annie's search, there was a big motor home with desks, chairs, and computers set up inside. And there was an officer of some kind in charge of operations, with people under him following his orders. Together they decided where to search and what means were to be used in the search.

All of them were very sympathetic to our experience even though they searched for missing people along the Columbia River Gorge all the time. Because of this, they knew the trails and had certified search and rescue teams who were specifically trained to search in this particular terrain.

The trails in themselves weren't that hard to navigate, but the second you went off trail, the terrain became insane. Imagine trying to walk on ground smothered in moss-covered boulders and fallen trees, with ferns three feet high to the left and right of you, and trees with leaves the size of a small watermelon all around you. The leaves were so large that at one point, my sister Leta and I held them up to our faces, in awe that one leaf completely concealed our faces and heads. In addition, you couldn't see the ground because the foliage was so dense, and you had no idea if you were walking on top of a boulder, on the side of one, or in between. It was unbelievable, like walking around in a giant's garden. It made me realize, when I first returned to Utah after being in Oregon, how brown and desert-like my hometown was. But the fact that the terrain off trail was so dense, with the most gnarly vegetation I've ever seen, meant each and every step had to be taken carefully.

That first day, we met in the trailer in the morning with the search and rescue officials to discuss the plans for the search for that day. At first, other than their trained professionals, the officials were adamant that they didn't want other searchers involved in the search. They were particularly worried that inexperienced hikers would get lost or hurt, as they had had some bad experiences working with friends and families of missing persons in the past. So they discouraged us from asking anyone to come help search.

After the initial conference meeting, we decided that Jon and Spencer would go with the search teams, and I would stay at base camp to field calls and interviews with the media, especially since my back and foot were not able to hike for hours on end on the gritty trails. This meant I did a lot of waiting around, wondering and questioning if the searchers had found Annie yet, or any clue of her whereabouts, but were not close enough to base camp to relay their findings. This also meant that I was available to be absolutely and sweetly inundated with texts and calls from family and friends expressing love and offering encouragement and prayers for Annie's safe return. So, as I sat in the rental car, waiting to hear any news, I texted some form of thank-you to one person after another.

I was so thankful for the outreach of love and support I felt. At the same time, I was completely numb and in shock. I had no emotional ability to give back to people, as far as being able to express gratitude and appreciation for their concern on our behalf. Even now, I can't recall everything that happened during the first search, or everyone I interacted with.

But the details I do remember were such a comfort to me. This included having Annie's roommate with me the entire time, for hours each day of the search. She was like a warm blanket, comforting, silent, supportive. In addition, the local stake president, President David Lake, was with me at base camp that whole first day. When I think of the kindness of this man to just hang out all day, interacting with me now and then, seeing if there was anything I needed, asking the Relief Society to bring us food, I'm truly humbled. Not only did he exude kindness, he was very respectful of those supervising the official search, not getting in their way or trying to take charge even though he was more than capable of doing so. It was as if his sole purpose for being there was to take care of me, and this touched me deeply.

Earlier that morning, we had been informed that there would be several dog teams searching. I was anxious for their arrival, because I had high hopes that the dog teams would be able to find Annie sooner than anyone else. But as the day wore on, I saw only one handler with his dog. This concerned me. Also, there didn't seem to be as many searchers as I had expected. We had been told there would be around 100 search and rescue people, but the people I saw didn't reflect those numbers. As time went on, I became increasingly worried we didn't have the search team necessary to find Annie.

I went to the trailer to inquire and found out from the search and rescue official that there was "another individual lost in the gorge" and the rescue resources had to be divided between the two search efforts.

At the time I believed finding Annie was more important than finding anyone else who might be lost in the area. But deep down I knew that wasn't the case, and I couldn't deny that the search and rescue officials were doing the very best they could, considering the circumstances.

When Jon returned from searching that first day, we discussed what we should do.

"I think it's time to ask for help, especially since there are so many people willing," I said.

With that, we asked for help from anyone physically capable who wanted to and could search. I don't remember exactly how we got the word out, but it included telling the local stake president, sending out texts to family and friends, and posting on Facebook and other social media outlets that we were ready for more aid in finding our daughter.

As the light began to fade and we ended the search on the first day, we gathered in the motor home and had another meeting, in which search leaders recapped what had been accomplished that day, including which areas and trails had been searched. Though much terrain had been covered, there was so much more to do.

Later, Jon, Spencer, Alec—Spencer's and Annie's good friend—and I got in our cars and drove to find something to eat. We found a little Italian restaurant, and as we walked in looking haggard, filthy, and careworn, acting as though we hadn't spent all day in the mountains looking for my lost daughter, I thought, "I wonder what we look like. What might people be thinking of us?" I felt as if I were living yet another surreal day.

After dinner, we made our way to a little hotel beside the gorge. Jon, Spencer, and Alec passed out immediately. But even though I was exhausted, I lay there awake, thinking of my children.

My twin boys, Chris and Jonny, were on missions in the UK, having departed the month before. And my youngest, Sarah, was at home with a friend whose family had taken her to St. George to try to get Sarah's mind off of what was happening with Annie and the search. But the trip wasn't working. Sarah was distressed beyond words, feeling isolated and alone. So, before I fell asleep, I called her. We didn't really speak, only cried and cried and cried, harder than we'd ever cried before, until we both fell asleep from exhaustion. Though we were hundreds of miles apart, expressing our grief together made me feel connected to Sarah, as if I were there holding her, comforting her in our sorrow.

The next day was Saturday. We got up early and headed to the base camp while the sun rose behind the clouds, since it had begun to rain again. As we pulled into the parking lot, I was blown away at the sight before me. There were multiple canopies set up, with tables and maps and people gathered around getting orders from another self-made search and rescue effort organized by the local members of the Church. The sight was a miracle—organized in one night's time. In addition, the new searchers were careful not to contradict or compromise the original effort in any way. A U.S. army general was organizing the search parties and giving them GPS coordinates in which to search. There were canopies set up with all kinds of things to eat and drink, being replenished on a regular basis throughout the day for all of the volunteers. I was overwhelmed at the generosity before me.

And then I saw three of my brothers: Jesse, Jake, and Dave.

"We came as fast as we could," Jake said, pulling me into a hug.

"Anything for our Annie," Dave said as I hugged him back, unable to say more than "Thank you."

"We're ready to go," Jesse said matter-of-factly.

Then I noticed all the climbing and rappelling equipment they had brought and realized that, with this gear, they would be able to search in areas some of the average hikers couldn't reach.

I was filled with such a profound love for these brothers of mine who had traveled all night, answering the plea Jon and I had given the day before for anyone to come and help look for Annie.

My youngest sister, Leta, arrived as well. She was one of the biggest supports to me during the entire first week of the search and into the following year, taking on many of the responsibilities that were on my shoulders. I'll forever love her for how much she emotionally carried me.

My mom was also so supportive at home, being actively involved by interacting with people on the websites (which I didn't even realize existed at the time) and keeping them updated and informed. Other siblings and in-laws who had lent their spouses to come search kept us constantly in their thoughts and prayers.

In addition, close friends, both Jon's and mine, arrived throughout the day. And besides the many friends and Church members who came to help, there were so many who were not of our faith and who didn't know us—people from all over the Gorge area—there to search for our daughter. Then I started to see members from our home ward, stake, and community, filing in all throughout the day. They were there to work, and they immediately got on search teams and headed into the mountains.

I can't even describe what this support felt like to us. Although I was unable to really interact with anyone in a very meaningful way, I was dumbfounded at the support we

Left: Brothers Jake and Jesse Anderegg, friend Alec Hales, son Spencer, and brother Dave Anderegg. Right: Sister Leta Anderegg Robinson, coordinating with one of the kind volunteers on the search.

received. I can still picture clearly the people's faces as they gathered around to get their assignments to head up the mountain and look for my daughter. I can still see them limping off the hill at the end of the day, and I can tell you that I will love these people for the rest of my life. I didn't know the people who organized everything locally. I was probably so thoughtless as I walked past people who had done so much for us, not even knowing it was them. To this day I still don't even know who to thank and how to thank them.

The fact that so many helped, all because a little girl was missing and her mom needed help finding her, truly humbles me. This beauty of people coming together with a Christlike love to serve and to help and to sacrifice for others, regardless of religious beliefs, amazes me. The goodness of humanity is a miracle.

The beauty of the organization of the Church is also a miracle. It is literally a huge family and safety net. When we're baptized, we promise to mourn with those who mourn and comfort those who stand in need of comfort. We really do that for each other. And in case we may become negligent in remembering to keep that promise, we are assigned to a few specific people, to actually take care of them. It doesn't matter where you are in the world, as a member of The Church of Jesus Christ of Latter-day Saints, there are members close by who will help you if you need help, who will feed you if you need food, who will give you a priesthood blessing if you need a blessing. Because the Church is your family, always there for you.

When I first arrived in my mission in Oslo, Norway, I was so freaked out to be in a strange country. I couldn't understand anything anyone said, it was practically dark all day long, and everything was freezing cold. It seemed like the locals hated Mormon missionaries and didn't want to have anything to do with us, and the subways were dark, underground, and had a strong odor of urine. I felt so scared, lonely, and homesick.

But when I went to church, though I still didn't know anybody, nor could I understand anything that was said, when the sacrament started, the old familiar warmth and assurance from the Holy Spirit came upon me. It filled me with peace and bore witness of truth. It testified of our Savior, Jesus Christ, and of the emblems we were taking in remembrance of Him, and I knew that I was going to be okay. This was the same Church of Jesus Christ as back home, with the same familial safety net. Even though I couldn't understand Norwegian, I could understand the Spirit. And it was like a warm blanket had enfolded me and told me I could bear testimony of Christ in this land that seemed strange. The feeling was familiar and safe and comforting.

Wherever you find the gifts of the Spirit manifest through priesthood ordinances, you will find a safety net waiting there to catch you, to save you, to help you. I wonder if sometimes, for those of us who have grown up in the Church, this is a blessing we take for granted because we've grown used to always having it.

That Saturday morning in the mountains in Oregon, I didn't take that blessing for granted. I was overcome with thankfulness and gratitude. And I still weep as I think of the goodness of people who came to our rescue that day. "Inasmuch as ye have done it unto one of the least of these my brethren, ye have done it unto me" (Matthew 25:40). I

Jon leading a group of searchers in prayer.

pray that the Lord will bless everyone who helped us, because I don't have the ability to adequately thank everyone. Their self-less sacrifice for us fills me with a desire to give my life in service to others for the rest of my days. I have never had a bucket list. But if I could choose, I just want to do whatever Heavenly Father directs me to do to help His children while I'm on the earth. I pray for the strength and the ability to do so.

Another thing that I was so grateful for during this time was the power of prayer. At the beginning of each day of searching, after people had received their assignments, we would gather in a circle in prayer to petition our Heavenly Father to please help us find our daughter. Jon offered one prayer that I felt was particularly significant in that it captured the essence of how we tried to face this experience. In his prayer, he said something like, "Heavenly Father, we know that Thou knowest exactly where Annie is right now. And we know that Thou couldst lead us to her immediately. We earnestly ask that Thou wilt answer the desire of our hearts and lead us right to her today. But if it isn't Thy will to do so at this time, we ask Thee to help us to not lose our faith in Thee and in Thy ability to answer prayers. Please help us to remember all of the times that Thou hast heard and answered our prayers. And please help us to never lose our faith in Thee, especially as we are struggling so much at this time with the sorrow and anxiety that we are feeling over the loss of Annie. Please strengthen our faith." I felt so grateful for the attitude of seeking to trust God throughout this experience. This trust was a continual source of peace that permeated the camp among all those who were involved in the search. And I was grateful for my husband, who sought to lead out in trying to have that attitude himself.

At the close of the third day of searching, the official search and rescue team withdrew from the search. Our daughter had not been found. But I couldn't blame these people. They had worked so hard for us—I can't even imagine what it must have cost to run such a search.

As we had our final meeting with the search officials, they recapped everything that had been done and expressed their condolences that they were not able to find our daughter. Then they commented on the other search and rescue stations that had been set up by our church next to theirs. They said, "We've never seen a better organized group of people in all our years of search and rescue. Your leaders are respectful and haven't hampered our efforts in any way. In fact," they continued, "your local church's efforts have been a huge asset. We have been able to work together in a way that really benefited the overall effort."

I then asked the leading official, "Are you familiar with The Church of Jesus Christ of Latter-day Saints?"

He smiled sheepishly and said, "I have family in Idaho who belong to the Church. Each year they put on a huge family reunion. I go to it every now and then. Every time I do, I'm amazed at how organized and well planned every bit of the reunion is." Then, looking around at the crowd, he added, "The search effort to find your daughter, put on by your church, reminds me a little bit of my family reunions." We all had a good laugh at this.

Laughter. You may wonder how anyone could laugh while going through something so horrific. The truth of the matter is, we just couldn't cry all day every day, especially when there was a monumental task to be performed. We had to dig deep and put one foot in front of the other and do what had to be done. And part of what we were doing was hiking through the mountains looking and yelling for Annie, all day long. I'm glad that there was laughter at times along the way.

With my siblings there, despite my physical limitations, I left the sanctuary of the rental car and got out on the trails with the search groups. Searching for my lost daughter in the most beautiful place imaginable was the most wonderfully bonding experience I could have ever had with my siblings. We reasoned together, we struggled up and over and under terrain together, we cried together, and we laughed together. I felt so much love and unity as we struggled physically, emotionally, and spiritually together. I imagined Annie looking down and being thrilled at all the connections and bonding that occurred during the search.

There were so many miraculous connections that were

made. One of them led to a marriage between a boy from Utah and a girl from Oregon who met while searching. Many people said they felt Annie on the trails with them, rejoicing in the fact that they were out in this beautiful part of God's earth.

Don't get me wrong: even though there was much that was good, searching for Annie was the most grueling, heartbreaking nightmare of my life. I've never experienced such drastic ups and downs testing my faith and hope in such a short period of time.

At one point, a woman with some kind of psychic gift, who had helped different police groups find abducted children, came on site. Being at our wit's end, and believing God could inspire anyone to help us to find Annie, we listened to what she had to say. She said that Annie was still alive and barely hanging onto life. She gave a direction in which she believed Annie was located. The sun was beginning to set, and it was getting cold. But Jon took off in a full sprint in the direction indicated, running up the river, yelling Annie's name at the top of his lungs. Despite our previous beliefs that Annie had already passed away, if there were any chance whatsoever that she was alive, Jon would kill himself to get to her.

But even as much as he wanted to find her, at one point, he thought he saw something that looked like skin, and he got the biggest pit in his stomach. Much to his relief, it wasn't skin, and it wasn't Annie. I think it would have been so hard for him to actually find her. It would have been hard for any of us to find her at that time in a near-death state—or dead and decomposing.

When the official search and rescue teams loaded up and drove away, Jon, Spencer, my siblings, and some ultra-committed searchers and friends milled around. We didn't know what to do. The official search was over, and we hadn't found Annie. Jon and I were completely empty. We couldn't even put a sentence together, let alone come up with a game plan as to what we should do next. Out of nowhere, our son Spencer stepped up and took over. He went to John Harding, a dear friend and former member of our stake presidency in Bountiful, and asked if he would take the lead in continuing the search.

John Harding was nothing short of an angel sent to us to carry us on. He agreed to take charge of the search, and Jon and Spencer stayed on with him for several more days. But I felt like I had to get home to Sarah, who was beside herself.

Knowing I would soon be leaving Oregon, I thought, "What will we do next? Where do we look? Where do we even find the strength to keep going?"

PART 2
How the Past Prepared Me for the Future

CHAPTER 6

Learning to Trust God in Family Life

As I look back on that first week in Oregon—discovering that Annie was missing and had possibly already passed into the spirit world—and knowing what happened after, with the month-long search, I realize that the Lord had tutored me and prepared me for that devastating time through years of experiences that had taught me to trust in Him and His plan for me and my family. Many of my trusting-in-God tutorials—chances to practice placing my trust in Him and His timing—occurred in my courtship with Jon, our marriage, and our early family life.

Shortly before I came home from my mission in Norway, Jon Schmidt's name came into my mind. This subtle thought turned into a persistent prompting telling me I needed to contact Jon when I arrived home. At the time, I hadn't seen any significance in the fact that Jon and I had both served missions in Norway. I realized later that it was a fun coincidence that we were called to serve in the same mission.

Regardless, upon my return from Norway, the prompting to contact Jon continued. I assumed this prompting was from the Holy Ghost, but if it was, I was baffled as to why it would be given. Jon and I had dated a bit before my mission, but things didn't click at the time, and I had no intention of calling him for the purpose of wanting him to ask me out. Yet the strong impressions persisted until I called him. We had a nice conversation about Norway and my mission, and then, as the small talk died down, Jon asked if I wanted to go do something sometime. When I agreed in kind of a hesitant way, Jon was completely confused as to why I had called him in the first place. We were both confused: dating each other was not what either of us was looking for. Jon had sent off a missionary whom he had every intention of waiting for. But when I reached out to him, he decided it wouldn't hurt to hang out a bit.

On our first post-mission date, we went to a water park with some friends. We had a blast and really enjoyed speaking Norwegian with each other. So we continued to go on dates, and I enjoyed being with Jon so much because he was such a good guy. He was funny and kind and respectful, and I loved talking with him. We would talk and talk for hours about all different kinds of topics. But mostly I loved our spiritual discussions about different doctrinal ideas.

From the get-go, spending time with Jon was a safe opportunity to date a fun guy without getting too attached. Our relationship so far was completely platonic. But as time went by and we spent more and more days together getting to know each other better, going on dates to firesides and parties and spending time with each other's families, it became harder for us to pretend we were only friends.

One Sunday night we went up to the Cliff Lodge at Snowbird Ski Resort and found a huge piano at the bottom of an open hall where the atrium ceiling overlooked the piano twenty stories below. Jon started playing the piano, and the music carried all throughout the atrium.

People came to the banisters on all different levels and looked down and listened to Jon playing. They made requests, and he put on a little impromptu concert. It was so much fun. I went up to the top level and was amazed at the beauty of the music as it rang all around me. Eventually everybody went to their rooms, and Jon and I were left alone on the piano bench. He picked me up and set me on his lap, and, with his arms reaching around me, he began making up a song for me.

I wrote in my journal that night, "Jon sang about the first time he ever saw me and how pretty he thought I was and how amazed he was to discover that I was also spiritual. He sang about how we'd dated a little but that he could tell I wasn't interested. But then he discovered how different I was from when we had dated before, emphasizing how, to him, I seemed humbler, loving, kind, and sweet. He told me how sincere he thought I was and that he truly loved me.

"Then he really kissed me for the first time, and I couldn't believe how beautiful it was. It was so tender and yet so intimate and loving. And what made the kiss even more special was that it felt like it had so much meaning. It was the most intimate and sensitive kiss I've ever experienced. It made me feel so much warmth and love for him, because he treated me like gold, like I was cherished."

After our date at Cliff Lodge, we spent tons of time together. We became closer and closer, growing emotionally and spiritually together, until we *both* acknowledged we loved each other. This made it harder and harder for me to be okay with Jon's insistence on waiting for his missionary friend. I had completely fallen in love with that redheaded boy.

All of a sudden, I was in a position to get hurt. And I thought, "No! I refuse to be hurt. I refuse to love anyone again until it is the boy I marry." I questioned and reasoned, "Why does Jon want to wait for his missionary friend? He must like her better than me. If so, then I'm going to bail and find someone else." But I couldn't. I had never found anyone as special as Jon before in my life. I couldn't just completely turn and walk away from him.

Feeling all of these emotions meant I really had to put my trust in God's will and timetable. I cared for Jon so much, but I wasn't completely sure I wanted to marry him. It scared me to death to think of marrying someone with a career as unstable as a piano player. That was definitely a serious consideration. Also, I remember thinking at the time, "Do I want my kids to have red hair? Is that what I really want?" It seems like such an insignificant and immature worry to have, but to my twenty-something self, this was one of my concerns. And I wondered, could I live with Jon forever? I never could have foreseen when we began dating that I would end up feeling the way I did for Jon. But, then again, Jon was perfect for me. So I decided to fast and pray and go to the temple to sort out my feelings.

Thankfully, at the temple I felt enabled to see things in an eternal perspective. That special day, I was filled with a hope and excitement when I thought about a life with Jon. I thought about living with someone who shared the same spiritual goals, and about how we could try to completely and unitedly dedicate ourselves to the work of the Lord, with a mutual desire to serve His children and to uplift each other. I knew I could lean on Jon and depend 100 percent on him spiritually. I realized I would not mind one bit to walk side by side with him, and that I would be comfortable and proud to have him be the patriarch for me and my family.

As I sought to trust, I was filled with a peace, and I felt confident everything would work out as it was supposed to. I could see the purpose behind Jon's prompting to wait for his missionary. This had been the means of allowing us to get close without any restraint. Without that, I don't think either of us would have ever let the ease of our relationship take place.

Since returning from my mission, I had prayed earnestly for the Lord to direct me to the right boy to marry, and even before I came home from my mission He put Jon into my head and kept prompting me to get ahold of him until I finally did. Talk about a loving Heavenly Father! I feel the Lord guided me along, exemplifying to me the truth of the Lord's words in 3 Nephi 13:8: " . . . for your Father knoweth what things ye have need of before ye ask him."

I left the temple feeling so good and peaceful about Jon. I called him and told him how happy I was, and that I knew everything would work out. I didn't tell him I thought we would get married, just about the peace I felt.

We continued to date, and Jon eventually received his own

good feelings about marrying me. In February of 1991 we were engaged, followed by our marriage the following June.

Trusting in God's timetable regarding my relationship with Jon was an actual test of my faith that reaffirmed to me that God knew if and when things would happen, and that I needed to find hope in the peace God had given me in the temple, come what may.

Our engagement picture.

Marriage was such a blessing in my life. I felt so close to the Lord, feeling so much joy and peace. The early months of marriage were also a time when I felt the Lord refining me in so many ways. I was able to see my weaknesses more clearly, and at times this was really painful. Yet, at the same time, I felt an increased power in my life to overcome some weaknesses quickly that I had struggled and wrestled with all through high school and college. I truly believe that I received increased spiritual power through entering into the sealing ordinance.

Looking back, I see that the importance Jon and I placed on seeking to become one with each other, and with the Lord, became a blessing that allowed me to grow and develop in a remarkable way. All this personal growth felt like a direct result of the growing unity I felt with Jon as we sought to unify ourselves with God. I believe this unity in our early marriage was a blessing that helped us to be able to stay unified when Annie went missing.

In time, our family of two grew as we were blessed with our first child, Spencer. So much of waiting for Spencer to join our family was filled with anticipation and preparation. One of the biggest feelings of anticipation we experienced was centered on wondering how my back would handle my pregnancy. With how limited I was in some physical areas, we had no idea what to expect. But we tried to be faithful in responding to a definite feeling that God wanted us to build a family, and so we trusted that my back would handle a pregnancy if it was the Lord's will.

Despite our worries, we looked at life as an adventure, and we were so excited to bring a new spirit into our family. Even though my back condition did become problematic, I have the greatest and most fun memories of the months leading up to Spencer's birth. Of that time, I wrote in my journal, "Today when we went grocery shopping, Jon walked around the store with me while I drove in the little handicapped cart. He did the craziest things, and we laughed our heads off. He got on the store intercom and called for 'Michelle Anderegg to the front, please. Michelle Anderegg to the front.'

"I told him, 'I'm Michelle Schmidt now.'

"But he said, 'I fell in love with the sexy Michelle Anderegg, and that's always who you'll be to me.'

"Most nights we lie in bed and laugh and laugh before falling asleep. And with Spencer sitting on my bladder, it is ten times as hard for me to control my bladder. Jon takes it as a personal compliment if I laugh so hard that I have to jump out of bed and run to the bathroom."

Eventually Spencer was born (on Jon's dad's birthday), and, despite experiencing continuous back pain, my body had handled pregnancy miraculously well.

Early motherhood was an adjustment. It was a time when my ability to trust God was again tested. I had never before felt such peace and purpose in my role as a woman, and I loved being a mother. But staying home with Spencer, while Jon spent all day and often into the night working on music, soon became very lonely. I had to learn and relearn to not feel sorry for myself as I suddenly found myself so completely tied to my baby. I quickly realized that motherhood was a crash course in learning to become selfless. I had to work to not be jealous each time Jon got to walk so freely out the door. We both had to work and sacrifice to make sure that I could also find ways to do things for myself to fill my well, like going to book club or getting to the gym. Having a child forced us to learn to sacrifice for each other in ways we hadn't considered before. In addition, our weekly date nights became essential in getting a break from parenting and having one-on-one time with each other.

Soon enough we felt we should have a second child. And, just like before, my back was in pain, but I continued to receive blessings that miraculously sustained me through the pregnancy.

One night, about three months into my pregnancy, before we'd had an ultrasound, I had a dream that I was pregnant with a little girl. In my dream I saw my daughter as a three-year-old. She was helping me with our new little baby boy. She had sandy blonde hair to her shoulders and big blue eyes. She seemed quiet, almost shy. She stared into my eyes for a long time, and I said to her, "I can't believe you're mine."

Upon waking, I recorded the dream in my journal and wrote, "We shall see if I'm having a girl. But I think I am, and her name will be Anna Catherine." We had an ultrasound a month or so later and found out we were having a girl, confirming what my dream and heart had already told me.

I was excited for Annie to join our family, but I was worried about delivering a baby around Christmastime. I've always thought Christmastime would be such an awful time to have a baby. But amazingly, it was a really special time of year to be pregnant. I thought so much about Mary going forth in faith, especially since it was her first baby—she must have been so scared and unsure. As I prepared the nursery for my baby, I would think of Mary not having any idea where she would deliver her baby. I thought of how she had to rely totally upon the Lord, not knowing how things would be for her. I felt so grateful for what we had, even as humble as our circumstances were. And I felt strengthened in my faith as I thought about the strength of Mary. She became a hero to me that month.

Annie joined our family on December 30, 1994, born on Jon's mom's birthday. About that experience I wrote in my journal: "At one point during the labor, when Jon had gone to get something to eat, I was in the delivery room all by myself. As I was lying there, all of a sudden, I felt a strong feeling of warmth, love, and joy. I felt like Annie and I were going to be really good friends. I felt so much love and happiness, and I felt the Spirit so strongly as I became excited for my life with my new best friend."

After Annie was born, I marveled at what a good-natured baby she was. She smiled real smiles all the time and brought me so much joy. She was much easier than my first baby had been. (Maybe I was a little bit better at being a mother than I had been the first go-round also.)

Feeling that my job as a mother was a sacred stewardship, I loved my opportunity to raise these two precious souls that God had sent to our family. But after Annie was born, there were times I felt inadequate and wondered if I was doing a good job. In addition, I really began to question the worth of the role of being a mother. At times it felt so boring and unimportant, even though I believed that raising children unto the Lord was one of the most important things I could do.

I began to feel a desire to find valiant female role models whom I could strive to emulate to find worth in the day-to-day routines of motherhood. My own mother was such a woman, but at the time I was searching for even more. I began to look at the women in my ward and neighborhood whom I could relate to, who had hormones and who sacrificed their bodies to bear children, who sat on the back row in church and wrestled sometimes alone with their children while their husbands conducted a meeting, and who did these things with joy, for the Spirit filled them with an eternal perspective.

As I cleaned up spills and changed diapers, I experienced

a spiritual crisis of sorts. I felt a strong desire to find validation of my seemingly insignificant daily lifestyle in motherhood. I trusted that the Lord could guide me through this spiritual dry spell, and so I turned to Him in prayer, asking Him to help me feel joy and purpose in my everyday life. I began to read and study about other Latter-day Saint women, looking to be strengthened by their examples. I think I would have loved to have been Sarah Kimball's friend. I read somewhere that she would go into the School of the Prophets to learn and talk about the gospel with the brethren. I decided that if I had another daughter one day, I would name her Sarah. I immersed myself in the scriptures and found strength to hang onto my faith despite my self-doubts. But I still could not shake the depression and guilt that I battled at times as I dreaded some of my daily routines. So I continued to ask the Lord for further inspiration and understanding.

As I prayed one day, a memory was brought to my mind of something that I had experienced just before I was to return home early from my mission because of health reasons. I had been praying because I was discouraged that I had to leave the mission field without feeling like I had done anything substantial, including baptizing anyone.

As I told the Lord these feelings, the words from the children's Primary song came to my mind: "I'm small, I know, but wherever I go the fields grow greener still" ("'Give,' Said the Little Stream," *Children's Songbook* [2002], 236).

As this memory came back to me, I felt a sweet peace come over me that Heavenly Father was aware of me and my life. I felt that, though I may have felt small, my little contributions could make a difference to the world in ways that He acknowledged and loved me for. I felt a greater sense of trust in Him and His plan for me and for all His creations. The Spirit filled me with a feeling that whether we are a nursery leader or Joseph Smith, our lives can be equally justified before the Lord.

I was so grateful to have this memory brought back to my mind, and so grateful to be able in that moment to have access to an eternal Heavenly Father and Savior to help me along, line upon line. Realizing Their great love for me filled me with a sense of worth and joy. I'm eternally grateful for this and many other similar times in my life when I feel I have definitely received knowledge and light, comfort and strength, through the grace of the Son.

Time went on, and two years later, we found out we were expecting again. I had had some forebodings that something about this pregnancy was going to be really hard. I wondered if the child I was carrying was going to have disabilities, or if he or she would be rebellious. I wasn't sure what the nature of the hardship would be, but I had a feeling of uneasiness.

One night, Jon and I went to the temple, where I felt particularly preoccupied about the pregnancy and my forebodings of hardship. As I sat in the temple, I suddenly felt this very enthusiastic and excited spirit communicate to my spirit.

It was a little girl, my little girl, bursting through the veil to tell me she was so excited to come to our family, she could hardly wait. But she told me she wasn't coming with my current pregnancy; she was coming after. She just wanted me to know that, even though my current pregnancy would be hard, I had to be sure to bring her into our family next. It was a sweet and even funny interaction.

Even before this experience, I knew I would have another

baby at some time, especially since my dream about Annie, seeing her as a toddler helping me with a baby boy. But because I had been unsure of the nature of the challenge of this baby, I asked for a couple of blessings from my dad, and they both said, "Everything will be fine with the pregnancy, everything will go smoothly. Your baby will be perfectly healthy."

Shortly after this experience we found out the nature of the hardship of the pregnancy. Upon having an ultrasound we discovered we were having twin boys. We were in shock.

I was very scared because having even one baby had been so hard. To think of jumping from two children to four was almost impossible to imagine. But then, during the commotion and shock of the results of the ultrasound and the feeling of being overwhelmed, I had the impression that this was no coincidence but actually a merciful way in which the Lord could entrust us with another baby in our family without my back having to endure one more pregnancy. The entire experience was so unique and special, I felt blessed to be pregnant with twins.

It is a very real and amazing sacrifice every time a mother chooses, with God, to bring another soul to earth and become a co-creator with Him. I remember being determined that I would seek to do all in my power to raise these two boys to be useful priesthood holders and to be as great a benefit to God's children as possible.

My boys remained healthy, and my pregnancy progressed smoothly. But being pregnant with twins was very painful. I experienced severe back pain almost the entire time, and I was not able to do simple tasks like washing the dishes or anything else without lying down periodically, taking breaks so my body could regain some strength for me to get back up again. Overall, the pregnancy was a very long haul, and there were times I had to work hard to maintain my sanity. As I was stretched to unbelievable limits, I would have claustrophobic attacks, and I'd want to scream, "Get me out of here!" It was a mental marathon.

The twins were born in October of 1997, and in February of 1998 I wrote in my journal:

"My pregnancy was miserable as my body stretched to unreal proportions as it fit 15 lbs. of baby. Jonny weighed 7.10 and Chris weighed 7.4.

" . . . the hardest part during the pregnancy was trying to deal with Annie. I could barely hoist myself around, and Annie turned into a nightmare. I hate to be so negative, but I have never had a worse time in my life. Annie became so awful and hard. I cannot tell you what she put me through. And I really do realize that most of it just was not her fault. Her mother, although physically present, slowly became unable to meet her needs in any way. As I was physically being pushed to limits where I thought I could bear no more, then Annie would come in and push and push and push until I really felt like I would lose it.

"I can say that in all those experiences where she did and does that, the battle has been mainly inside myself to be patient and long-suffering. But there have been those times when I have lost it with her. And then I sob and sob, because I feel like such an awful mother. I have no idea what to do with her. A strong-willed child is putting it lightly. I really do love her more than I can say, but she has been the trial of my life, in addition to the birth of my twin boys.

"My little Jonny and Chris have been my easiest babies yet. But there are still two of them. It has been a living nightmare. I simply cannot describe how awful.

"I can barely remember anything specific I have done except for constantly run to try to meet the needs of one of my children. Spencer has been seriously neglected. Two babies demanding all kinds of around-the-clock attention, and Annie pushing me up the wall at every turn. There has been nothing left over for Spencer. He's acted up in school, fighting with the other kids. I am always demanding him to take care of himself. . . . He so rarely asks for something. But it seems like when he does that it is just more than I can take. And so, I get upset at him for asking for a drink of milk."

Within all of this family craziness, Jon was trying to do his first self-produced Christmas concert. He was stressed out of his mind. It felt like I spent all of November and December caring for four children all by myself. Though I was married and had some help from our extended family, I felt so overwhelmed, and I really struggled with depression during this time.

Jon's concert came and went, and thank heavens it was successful. We actually made a little money. It was the first time, ever, that we had made money on his Christmas concert. But Jon was so stressed that when he got on stage and began playing his first number, his fingers were completely numb. They felt like they had pins and needles in them, making it so he couldn't feel his fingers while he played "Waterfall." Luckily the song must have been in his muscle memory, because the fingers took over and played for themselves. He has no memory as to how he made it through that first number. He just prayed for help and was able to pull out of it.

I had four babysitters for the night. One was at home with Spencer and Annie, and three were in a dressing room backstage with the twins. I nursed the babies before the show and again during intermission. I had pumped bottles, brought swings, and packed all the diapers and other things we would need to care for two infants. It was quite the production I put on myself.

Jon's Christmas album sold really well. After we paid all of our bills, there was just a little left over to buy a dishwasher. I loved my dishwasher more than life itself. When I was feeling most depressed, I would think about my dishwasher.

After the concert, the December madness didn't slow down. Jon played at all kinds of engagements and was gone almost all the time. And when he *was* around, we were frantically trying to get the Christmas shopping done. Jon and I simply felt in over our heads, struggling to stay afloat.

The twins, me, Spencer, Annie, and Jon.

By the time January rolled around, I was a crumpled-up mess. I had reached my limit. I would scream and shake in my dreams. I wanted to die.

We decided to postpone as many career pursuits as possible for about a year because I needed Jon's help at home so desperately. Also, Jon got some people to come over to do whatever I needed. We paid them hardly anything, but they came two to three times a week for two hours at a time. They usually just cleaned my kitchen and held a baby so I could shower. (I was going four days at a time without showering, so that helped a lot.)

A couple of months later, Annie caught a really bad virus. She was down for about four days before she pulled out of it. Then I noticed the babies were getting sick. The doctor said they had RSV, but that they looked like they were doing tolerably well with it. We were sent home with a nebulizer machine to do breathing treatments ourselves for them. Though the treatments seemed to help Jonny some, Chris got worse and worse until we finally took him to the ER, where we found out the virus was shutting his lungs down so that he was unable to breathe. He was put on oxygen and admitted to the hospital.

The hospital was so overcrowded with children suffering from RSV that they didn't have a room to put us in. They set up a crib in a utility closet room. I slept about two hours that night, while Jon went home at 2:00 a.m. to relieve the neighbor who was watching Spencer and Annie. I hated it at the hospital, especially because I had Jonny with me since I was still nursing. I kept pushing to go home, but Chris was so sick that they didn't want us to leave yet. Eventually, because I was in a closet with two babies, the hospital released us. Besides, with Chris on oxygen and on antibiotics, there really wasn't anything more they could do.

The following week was honestly the worst week of my life to that point. It seemed like Chris was only getting worse, and it was killing me. Jonny was sick and fussy as well, though at least he could breathe. But Chris became so lifeless. Of this experience I recorded in my journal:

"I hardly slept that week. I spent night after night making sure Chris was breathing, giving him nebulizer treatments, and suctioning his nose. One night his struggle to breathe seemed to increase as he became more and more lifeless. I kept taking his temperature and it continued to go up. I was wracked with worry as I spent the night in their room watching over them. Suddenly I realized that Chris was slowly slipping away. I had just taken his temperature and it had gone up to 106, and I had the distinct feeling that he was losing this battle. I knew there was nothing more they could do at the hospital for him besides what I was doing. I was desperate. I knew there was only one person who could save my baby, and that was God.

"I had prayed and prayed throughout his sickness, but as I dropped to my knees next to the rocking chair, I prayed like I had never prayed before in my life. I begged the Lord to let my baby live. I wrestled with the idea that it may be His will that Chris pass away. I wrestled and struggled with this idea and I wrestled with my willingness to submit to the Lord if it was His will to take Chris. I reasoned and struggled in prayer until I felt like I got to a place where I thought I could mean it when I said that if it were His will to take Chris, then I would submit and trust His plan. And after I felt like I had sufficiently submitted my will as well as I could, then I began to plead in faith that He might let Chris live. I told the Lord if there was any way that it was not His absolute will to take Chris, then I was going to fight for his life with all that I possessed. And even as Lucy Mack Smith, mother of Joseph Smith, would kneel in great faith before the Lord on behalf of her children, even so I would do the same. I knew that the prayer of a mother could have great power. I began to analyze my faith and the amount of power and confidence before the Lord that I possessed to be able to draw upon the power of heaven to heal my child.

"How much faith and power did I really have? I thought about the Lord's words, ' . . . for verily I say unto you, If ye have faith as a grain of mustard seed, ye shall say unto this mountain, Remove hence to yonder place; and it shall remove; and nothing shall be impossible unto you.' I thought to myself, 'Surely I have as much faith as the size of a mustard seed. I know I have a mustard seed amount!' I have tried so hard to have faith and to trust in the Lord. As I thought about my faith, I absolutely KNEW that I had at least that much faith.

"And so, I went before the Lord with all of the power and confidence and faith that I possessed and exercised that faith in behalf of my baby. I exerted all that I had, all that I possessed. And then in exhaustion I fell asleep as I simply then tried to submit to the Lord, even as a child doth submit to his father."

Chris lived through the night and slowly began to get better. It wasn't until a month or so later that I realized his improvement began that night.

The thing I have realized since then is that our faith is not something that we use to get our way. Our faith isn't in outcomes, as Elder Bednar has taught (see "Accepting the Lord's

Will and Timing," *Ensign*, August 2016). Rather, our faith is in God the Eternal Father and in His Son, Jesus Christ. The more our knowledge increases of Them and Their reality, Their loving kindness and Their omnipotence, the more ability we have to obtain Their help in the things we are struggling through on this earth. That is why Shadrach, Meshach, and Abed-nego could tell King Nebuchadnezzar, when he was threatening to throw them into the fire, "If it be so, our God whom we serve is able to deliver us from the burning fiery furnace, and he will deliver us. . . . But if not, . . . we will not serve thy gods, nor worship the golden image which thou hast set up" (Daniel 3:17–18). They knew in whom they trusted. They knew their God and their Deliverer, Jesus Christ. And I believe that when you know Heavenly Father and Jesus Christ, you know you can trust Them. If They let you burn, or if They let your child die, you can trust that it was either Their will, for a purpose that you cannot see at the time, or that They will bless you that all things will work together for your good. You can trust that They will compensate because They love you. They will refine, purify, and make holy your most heart-wrenching sacrifices. You can trust Them because you have tasted of Their goodness.

As I try to explain these things that I feel are so valuable, I hope not to give the impression that I've mastered them myself. Far from it. But I can say that I've learned these things to a degree that I can testify they are true. And I've also felt myself increase in my ability to trust in these truths when faced with challenges. Each new challenge and hardship comes with unique circumstances that throw me for a loop. But the more times I trust in the Lord, the more experience I have with His ability to guide and deliver. The more experience I have with His ability to guide and deliver me, the more quickly I'm able to turn to Him in times of crisis.

Jon and I were so thankful to have a foundation of faith in Jesus Christ to sustain us when we lost Annie, when it felt like everything else was crumbling about us. We feel like we were able to stand on Him. He was our rock and our foundation. He carried us. He didn't leave us comfortless. I am grateful to be able to share that testimony without hesitation, with all my heart.

In time, the hardships of our early child-rearing years became memories. In 2001 we moved to Davis County, Utah, where we opened a new chapter in our lives. Our oldest was eight, Annie was five, the twins were three, and our fifth child was due in July of that year. The years we lived in Davis County were some of our happiest, as we did the bulk of raising our small family there.

"Blankey game" on the tramp.

Jon spent countless hours dragging the kids around the trampoline on a blanket, an activity lovingly known as "blankey game." There were huge blow-up-slide birthday parties, bike riding around the block, playing "Annie-I-Over" around the house, wild dancing to Jon playing the piano, lots and lots of Little League, junior high, and high school football, basketball, and baseball games, dance lessons and recitals and competitions and conventions, singing and piano lessons, exciting Christmas mornings, countless friends in and out of the house at all hours and through every day of the week, and lots of trick shots in the backyard. Even though life continued to be laced with challenges, I look at that time as the most rewarding and golden in my life. Those years of raising our family were filled with so much joy and laughter and faith-promoting growth, they helped prepare us to face losing and searching for Annie.

CHAPTER 7

Learning to Trust God in Building a Career

In addition to the Lord tutoring us through the ups and downs of early family life, He truly taught us to trust in Him through building a career in music.

When I told my mom I was marrying a musician, I thought she was going to die. But choosing to pursue a career in music was not a decision we made lightly.

Jon had always loved to play the piano, and he grew up entertaining friends and classmates throughout his high school years. He was even offered a piano performance scholarship in the music program at the University of Utah, but he turned it down because he really didn't want to be a full-time musician. He had seen people chase their music dreams, seen the struggle a music career put their families through, and wanted no part of it. He had decided to major in English instead, get an MBA, and go into some type of business.

But as his mission was coming to a close, he had an exit interview with his mission president, who asked what he planned to do when he got home.

"I plan to get an MBA," Jon said.

This mission president, who was also an ordained patriarch, asked Jon about his music.

Somewhat flippantly Jon replied, "I actually want to feed my family."

His mission president sat there in silence for a few moments, then said, somewhat sternly, pointing at the ceiling, "Do not neglect the gift the Lord has given you! I just told you something!"

Jon came away from this interview with a feeling he should be more attentive to his music, but he was still not convinced he needed to make it a career.

After his mission, Jon continued to get requests to play the piano at a variety of different venues as the demand for his music increased. A girl whom Jon had dated gave him a gift of a recording session. She took him to a recording studio to record several songs and put them on a cassette tape. Shortly thereafter he had an opportunity to play a benefit concert at his former high school. He brought along copies of his tape to see if anyone would be interested in buying them. To his great astonishment, he completely sold out of every single cassette. This got him thinking maybe there would be an audience for his solo piano music.

So he decided to go into debt to make his very own CD. This was pretty much a leap of faith because in 1990 he didn't know of any independent artists who had their own CDs. Sure, there were the big-name artists who were signed with major record companies, and in the LDS market there were some local artists, but as far as we knew, they were with some sort of record label and were not independent artists. At the time, it was a pretty gutsy move for Jon to produce his own CD. But Jon felt that because there was enough demand for his music, he would make back what it cost. He produced his first CD that year, titled *August End*.

We had both graduated with our bachelor's degrees, and it was time to decide what to do next. We prayed and prayed about Jon's career, and we felt absolutely prompted to give Jon's music career a try, at least for one year. This meant he peddled his CD to stores on consignment, tried to drum up any playing engagements he could, and taught piano lessons in order to ensure we got by. He played at a couple of concerts. And though we didn't make much from these concerts, each playing engagement was an opportunity for exposure.

At the end of that first year, after much fasting and prayer, we again felt we should continue on and pursue Jon's music

Jon's first CD, August End.

career for one more year. But as we began having children and our expenses increased, this decision to continue in music became more challenging and demanded more and more faith.

There was one time after Spencer was born when finances were particularly hard, and I completely broke down and cried and cried. I had a definite feeling I wanted to be a stay-at-home mother, and I was trying to accept the craziness of Jon being gone all the time working on a new CD in the morning, teaching piano lessons in the afternoon, and then working on his CD again all night.

Money was really low that month. The bills just kept coming, and I didn't know how we'd pay them. We had reached a point where we usually had a lot of playing engagements to supplement the piano lesson income, but that month we didn't have any added income, and we weren't making it.

Finally, Jon told me to take money out of savings to pay the bills. I really fought against doing this because it meant I would spend in one month what it took three months to save. But I finally had to. I wrote in my journal that month, "I'll have to trust in the Lord and not have anxiety."

And yet, I didn't know if we would ever make it. I didn't know if we'd ever be able to afford a house. I didn't even know if we'd ever be able to afford to buy clothes when we needed them. But I decided to keep praying and to trust that the Lord would help us. He had already helped us so much. We had always found the money to pay for the things we really needed. So, with Jon working as hard as he could, I had to leave the rest in the Lord's hands. I was slowly learning that living a life of faith instead of a life of anxiety led to greater peace.

At the end of that year, we again prayed and fasted to

know if music was the career path we should follow. And, despite the financial struggles, we again received the answer to continue forward.

Jon's playing engagements increased, including an opportunity for him to play a solo concert produced and aired on a local television station, which gave him a lot of publicity. As a result, he also had a huge full-page picture and write-up in the *Deseret News,* which helped with exposure as well. In addition, he received an invitation to play in a Utah Symphony sponsored summer concert at Deer Valley. Although he was just the opening act, we were again thrilled with any exposure he could get.

What was so frustrating was that none of these successes had resulted in any significant financial increase, which meant we still had no idea how we would make it each month. At the time I was worried about how we would afford a second baby. It was especially hard for me to watch other friends getting to a point where affording doing things was not so hard for them when it still was for us.

I shared with Jon all of my concerns, and we talked about how faith can be, and had been, an incredible power in our lives. The Lord had promised in several blessings that we would have sufficient for our needs, and we did. Talking about these things together was an opportunity for us to strengthen one another in our convictions and trust in the Lord, and we again felt a strong confirmation that we should continue in our efforts, and that the Lord would provide for us.

We both felt a strong desire, and considered it our source of greatest satisfaction, to raise children unto the Lord, and we believed that He would give us the ability to do so. We determined that what we needed to do was have the faith to ask for grace, the enabling power, to help us with three things: (1) to have enough income to provide for our family, (2) to have the strength to continue striving to overcome our weaknesses, and (3) to feel sure we were doing what the Lord wanted us to do. Thankfully, we were able to trust that He would provide and that He would sustain. We had faith in this. We felt that if we were seeking to fulfill His purposes, then we could ask for His help with full confidence that He would hear our prayers and guide our lives.

We read a scripture in Hebrews 13:5–6 that strengthened us at the time, which I then wrote down in my journal: "Let your conversation be without covetousness; and be content with such things as ye have: for he hath said, I will never leave thee, nor forsake thee. So that we may boldly say, The Lord is my helper, and I will not fear." We trusted in these promises.

At one tough point, after a concert had not gone as we had expected, Jon's dad, Werner, gave Jon a blessing in which he was told that the Lord loved him greatly because his desires were just and righteous. Then he said, "All of your righteous desires will be fulfilled, and you will be greatly blessed. You must have patience in this. It is not easy to have patience. But it is easy to pray for patience."

On another occasion we borrowed money from our savings to have enough money for a down payment on a house. The money we used had been saved to pay our taxes, but we were expecting a royalty check that we figured would cover what we had borrowed, so we weren't worried about taking from our savings.

We waited and waited for the royalty check to come. It

was way past the time when it should have arrived. When it did finally come, it was about a sixth of what we had expected. What had happened was that our record company had been sold from one president to another, which caused an oversight in keeping the stores stocked with Jon's product. All of a sudden, we did not have the money we needed to pay our taxes. This news was devastating to us. We were in shock.

We were both depressed, and neither of us could console the other. It was one of the lowest days I can remember in our marriage. We felt hopeless and discouraged, and again we wondered if it was time for Jon to give up music and go into some other business. I knew I needed help, some answers. So I went to the Lord.

And even though I didn't feel like it, I sat down and made myself read the most recent conference issue of the *Ensign*. The article I read was on tithing. I already had a strong testimony of tithing, but hearing the promises again helped to renew my faith and trust in the Lord that He would help us.

Quoting President Heber J. Grant, Elder Dallin H. Oaks said, "I appeal to the Latter-day Saints to be honest with the Lord and I promise them that peace, prosperity, and financial success will attend those who are honest with our Heavenly Father" (*Teachings of Presidents of the Church: Heber J. Grant* [2002], 126).

As I read, I had a peaceful calm come over me that I could trust in these promises given through one of the Lord's true messengers. I couldn't foresee how, but I prayed for the faith to believe that He would help us.

I poured my heart out to the Lord, explaining all the different areas where we would need financial help. We needed more than just the money for taxes. I was expecting Annie at the time, and I was worried about needing a bigger car as well. How would we ever have enough money?

After my prayer, as I pondered, I had a spiritual impression. In my journal I recorded: "In my mind's eye I saw my married daughter coming to speak with me and Jon, and she was asking for money to get out of debt.

"The me in my vision said, 'We have plenty of money and the means to bail you out, but we shouldn't just hand the money over to you to solve your problems. If you don't struggle and learn to turn to the Lord for help and guidance, you will never come to know the Lord as you need to. I love you more than my own life. It hurts me to see you suffer. But it is only through struggling through sorrow that you will be able to grow in faith and be able to reach your full potential. More than anything, I want you to reach your full potential.'"

As the me in my vision said "potential," instantly the meaning of that entire speech to my daughter hit me. I knew the Lord had counseled me, just as I would have counseled my own daughter.

When I shared this experience with Jon, we knew the Lord was aware of us and our situation and what we were experiencing. We also knew this experience was a means through which we would be able to come closer to Him. That knowledge, in itself, made the whole financial trial seem worthwhile.

And so we moved on, with Jon working his heart out to produce music while I did my best to manage whatever money came in. Our income continued to be extremely sporadic, so it was virtually impossible to budget. It literally felt like we pled for and lived on manna. Each month and each year we had to pray for ideas for compositions, pray for playing engagements, and pray for doors to open that would provide income. As a result, and of necessity, we relied on miracles.

In the fall of 1995 we were trying to decide where to do Jon's next concert. We were scared since the last concert at Kingsbury Hall hadn't been as successful as we had hoped. We toyed with all kinds of ideas, considering doing four shows at a place that seated fewer people than Kingsbury Hall. We talked through all the options, over and over. But our greatest fear was that no one would come, especially since Jon hadn't done a big, self-sponsored concert for two years. We fasted and prayed and asked the Lord to guide us and open the doors for us, knowing all things were possible with Him.

Then one night shortly thereafter, Jon couldn't sleep, so he went and sat on the couch in the living room. He looked out the window at all the lights sparkling across the Salt Lake Valley, and the thought came to his mind, "There are so many people out there who have never heard of you. If they knew about your music they would love it. It is time for you to think bigger."

After Jon told me about his impression, we decided to rent the Capitol Theater. We were a little scared, but we decided to "think big."

A few weeks later we received a call from the Capitol Theater. The Broadway show then playing wanted to extend, so they bumped us off our date. However, as a consolation, they would give us Abravanel Hall for the same price. Abravanel Hall? The most prestigious hall in Salt Lake City, where the Utah Symphony performed—which seated twice as many as the Capitol Theater?

We were terrified! We never would have thought that big on our own. To make a long story short, we gave away a huge number of complimentary seats because we were so afraid no one would show. Regardless, Jon worked like an absolute madman promoting the concert. So did I. It consumed us. And since we were scared to death, we kept praying and working.

The night of the show, when I got to Abravanel Hall, people were flocking in! The lobby was filled, and the lines to get tickets were enormous. It was amazing! It felt like everyone who knew Jon was there and happy for him. We felt so grateful for the support of our local community. The house was almost completely filled—at least, it looked full to us. We were amazed. Never in our wildest imaginations would we have chosen Abravanel Hall. Once again, we felt extremely blessed.

However, we barely made any money because we did a lot of dumb things like spending too much on promotion. But we learned a lot. I wrote in my journal, "We're going to see if we can make some money next time." Overall, the experience with Abravanel Hall left us optimistic.

The next year, Jon produced his first sheet-music book. We were very hopeful it would be another stepping-stone along our path to being financially stable. Jon had a gut feeling that the sheet-music book was going to be a success, and he felt a lot of inspiration as he created it. I was hopeful and believed in the impressions Jon received. But so far, everything Jon did took so much of our guts, sweat, and tears, and as yet seemed to produce very little money to live on.

In addition, we were facing the fact that our record company was on the brink of going under. We didn't know what would happen to us; we just kept praying the Lord would guide us.

Pretty soon Jon was planning his next Abravanel Hall concert. Knowing how hectic the preparation would be, I was afraid of failure and full of apprehension concerning the outcome.

I remember praying earnestly for the concert to be a success, so much so that I wanted the Lord to just give me my way. Then I tried to submit my will to the Lord's. I wrote in my journal, "If the concert is a complete flop and Jon's career suffers greatly, then so be it. I must learn to be submissive." I thought often of the early Saints in the Church and of some of the crazy hard trials they endured. Thinking of their strength and faith bolstered my own resolve to be faithful and trusting.

The second Abravanel Hall concert came and went, and in many ways it was a huge success. The concert went absolutely great, and Jon did such a good job. I was so proud of him. But financially, the concert was a huge failure. We didn't sell as many tickets as we had hoped, and after all the promotional expenses we had put into it in anticipation of selling more tickets, we ended up in the hole by a considerable amount. We were sick and in absolute shock. We didn't know what to do. Again, we turned to the Lord in desperation. This time we found great comfort in reading in Mosiah 24, where it says:

" . . . so great were their afflictions that they began to cry mightily to God. . . . And . . . the voice of the Lord came to them in their afflictions, saying: Lift up your heads and be of good comfort, for I know of the covenant which ye have made unto me; and I will covenant with my people and deliver them out of bondage. And I will also ease the burdens which are put upon your shoulders, that even you cannot feel them upon your backs, even while you are in bondage; and this will I do that ye may stand as witnesses for me hereafter, and that ye may know of a surety that I, the Lord God, do visit my people in their afflictions. . . . And they did submit cheerfully and with patience to all the will of the Lord . . . for they were in bondage, and none could deliver them except it were the Lord their God" (Mosiah 24:10, 13–15, 21).

We related so much to the situation of bondage in which these people in the Book of Mormon suddenly found themselves. Like them, we had no idea how to deliver ourselves from it. But as we read the scripture, we felt that the same promises the Lord gave to them were being extended to us. We felt that the Lord was telling us to be comforted and trust Him, and that He would ease this heavy burden we suddenly felt weighing down upon us. In addition, we were given the enabling idea that there was actually a great purpose in this trial, one that would give us future power and ability to testify of the Lord and to stand as witnesses of Him and His capacity to deliver us. We didn't know how or when we would be delivered, and we knew it might be the Lord's will that we remain in bondage for a period of time. But trusting in this scripture helped us to believe that He would make our burdens light so we could bear them with ease and someday testify of His goodness.

Regardless of the peace and strength we found from reading this scripture, this overwhelming setback caused us to revisit the same question of whether pursuing music was the right path for us. We questioned if we had even been correct in doing the concert in the first place. Suffering a loss of this magnitude made us seriously consider a career change, and Jon began earnestly looking into other career choices. We both felt that we needed some pretty clear and definite guidance from the Lord.

In response to our pleadings for such guidance, we received a couple of strong and undeniable promptings that encouraged us to keep going. One of those came to Jon as he was flying to Virginia to play an EFY concert. As he left that morning, he felt inspired to grab a random *Ensign* magazine from our coffee table to read on the plane. As he opened it, he flipped right to an article by Elder M. Russell Ballard written to the artists of the Church. The article spoke about the vital need for worthy and inspired artists to offer positive and uplifting alternatives to things in the world that degraded and tore down. It said music was a universal medium that crossed language barriers and enabled people throughout the world to experience feelings from the eternal. As we talked about the fact that Jon had picked up this *Ensign* and read this article right at the time we were seeking for answers on this topic, we both felt like this was no coincidence.

Another experience at this time that felt like a push to continue with music came from a very special blessing Jon received from his dad.

Jon's dad is a humble, five-foot immigrant from Germany who lived through World War II. Both he and Jon's mom are second-generation members of the Church, and they experienced amazing miracles throughout the war that left them with great faith. Though Jon's dad is small in stature, he is a spiritual giant. At this time of great questioning concerning Jon's career, Jon asked his dad to join us in a special fast that would conclude with him giving Jon a blessing seeking guidance and inspiration for our career.

In his thick German accent, Werner began his blessing in a very typical father's way. Then he paused, and as I listened, it felt like he began to literally prophesy. He said, "Jon, my son, you need to continue to pursue music because the Lord has a plan for your music. Your music is needed in Germany. It is needed in Japan. It is needed in South America, and all over the world."

After the blessing, we all stared at each other in disbelief. Werner said, "I had no intention of saying those things, but they came to me with such conviction and power." That was a power we all felt.

We sat there and marveled because we literally had no idea how in the world that blessing could ever be fulfilled. But Werner assured us, and was unable to deny, that the blessing he gave was what he was supposed to say.

Jon with his parents, Werner and Lieselotte Schmidt.

Receiving this encouragement from the Lord that Jon's pursuing this career was His will gave us the confidence to then plead in great faith for His help in delivering us from the overwhelming bondage of debt we found ourselves in. We began praying for the exact amount of money we needed to get out of debt. We had no idea where the money would come from. But we figured we would pray for a certain sum one month and then the rest the next month. We put our whole trust in the Lord and begged for help.

A few days later we received a check in the mail from Deseret Book for Jon's new sheet-music book he had recently produced. We were expecting a check, but we had no idea it would be as much as we received. This was a huge blessing and answer to our prayers. And then the same day Deseret Book put in another big order for more sheet-music books.

Also, so many people—the newspapers and radio stations, for example—were so kind in working out payment plans. FM100 even had Jon play some corporate functions in exchange for what we owed for promotion. In addition, Abravanel Hall agreed to give us a discount.

We didn't have all the money we needed immediately, but it was a miracle to watch the Lord answer our prayers bit by bit, which He continued to do over the next several months. As we had bills come due, we would "somehow" come up with the money necessary to pay them. We absolutely see it was nothing short of a miracle and a gift from God.

As I sat paying the last of the concert bills and saw that we had just barely enough to pay off our debts, I began to cry and prayed out loud, "Thank you. Thank you so much, Heavenly Father, for delivering us." I couldn't believe we had made it.

The blessing and goodness and answer to our prayers was so obvious it made me weep. How could we ever survive without our trust in and utter dependence upon the Lord? He had been so good to us. He even blessed us with a little extra for Spencer's birthday. I was so thankful. There was no adequate way to express it.

As I pondered upon these events, I realized that it was wisdom in the Lord that He had kept us in our humbled position, one that had enabled us to grow and learn many spiritual things. And I felt a complete feeling of peace, and even gratitude, for the things we had suffered. I truly felt a desire to testify as much as I could of God and of His power of deliverance.

Even with this miracle of deliverance, it just didn't seem like we would ever make enough to get ahead. We just prayed and somehow scraped by month after month. And yet, I knew the Lord fulfilled all of His promises, and I believed with all my heart that He could fulfill this promise given to us in Jon's dad's blessing. I could not deny the miracle we had received

Jon's famous upside-down piano playing.

throughout the year following the second Abravanel Hall concert. Jon had worked his hardest and we had exercised our faith the best we could, and we had been able to meet every awful, horrible deadline. We continued to be delivered miraculously every single month. We literally survived as if on manna from heaven. And all that God asked of us was that we put our trust in Him.

However, even with our faith, this was not the end of our financial trials.

When we moved to Davis County in 2001, we were faced with one of the hardest financial trials we had yet encountered. We discovered that money had been embezzled from us, which meant that, unbeknownst to us, we hadn't paid our taxes for a period of five years. Because we had trusted and believed that our taxes were being paid when they weren't, we were judged completely negligent and liable for the taxes owing and the penalties accrued. This tax burden became one of the hardest and most crushing financial weights that we have ever borne. For almost ten years we carried this heavy burden of trying to dig ourselves out of this financial pit. I prayed and pled with the Lord for years to somehow deliver us from this financial bondage that we again found ourselves in.

Luckily, true to Jon's dad's blessing, Jon's solo piano career was booming. There was a young couple, Carl and Emily Sandquist, who said they felt a definite inspiration to partner and take a role in the progress of his career as if it were part of their life mission. They were literally angels to us; they helped Jon's career continue to grow, helped produce the music books, and helped manage and run everything with us. This was such a blessing because our family was growing, and as it did, my involvement in the hands-on work of the career became less and less.

Jon continued to produce CDs and sheet music, developed a note-reading method that he shared through teacher workshops, did composing workshops, and played for almost every fund-raising, corporate, church, or private event that there ever was or ever would be in Utah. Some weeks he would play every night of the week. Several big shows had become reliable annual staples. Quite often Jon's events had him traveling out of state and even sometimes internationally. But Christmastime was by far the busiest.

I used to dread every Christmas, as the stress from putting on his yearly Kingsbury Hall Christmas show—along with performing every other night of December and trying to make a happy Christmas for our own children—made us nearly crazy. I couldn't wait until December was over and I could feel peace in our home again. We were grateful for the work, but it was a very busy, stressful, and demanding time of life.

At this time Steven Sharp Nelson began to come into the picture. Jon and Steve had gone to the same high school, but they were eleven years apart in age and so didn't know each other from school. In high school, Steve began playing with Peter Breinholt, and Jon was immediately taken with Steve's abilities and talent at such a young age. Eventually, Jon began asking Steve to add his cello genius to numbers in Jon's shows. It quickly became evident that Steve was much more than just a great cellist. He was quick-witted and had a comedic knack that was uncanny. The more Steve played with Jon, the more we were in awe of his abilities. Soon Steve became a regular in the yearly Kingsbury Hall Christmas show and other shows, and we grew to love him like a brother. He was so positive and fun-loving, and he would chase and play hide-and-seek or tag with our kids backstage. They grew up calling him "Uncle Steve." Even our children's friends called him that.

During all of this, Jon was always trying to discover new ways to keep the career growing. He and Carl Sandquist spent lots of time researching new markets and the quickly changing trends in the music industry. Jon was not afraid to try new things and was ever seeking to promote the eight albums and seven books of sheet music he had created. Jon and Carl got Jon's music on MP3, imeem, MySpace, CD Baby, Pandora, and iTunes when they were first becoming popular. They uploaded his music to YouTube in its early days before most people even knew what YouTube was.

Then, in 2009, Jon had an unexpected video idea for YouTube. He and Steve worked up a cover of Taylor Swift's "Love Story," with Steve playing the cello in unusual ways as well as playing the kick drum at the same time. Then Jon got the idea to have the Taylor Swift song morph into "Viva la Vida" by Coldplay. A friend of Jon's filmed Jon and Steve playing their version of this song in a local piano store. We had no idea what to expect when we released it on YouTube. As the weeks went by, and we watched this song go viral and inch up toward a million views, we freaked out. It was the most exciting thing ever. We had never seen anything like it. We became addicted to reading the comments that came in. People from all over the world were listening to Jon's music—and loving it! It was especially intriguing to us that the video spread like wildfire in Malaysia. The YouTube success was probably the most exciting thing we had experienced in Jon's career to date.

So, even though YouTube was so new, we quickly realized that it could be the means of spreading Jon's music to a worldwide audience, as Werner's special blessing had promised. We felt like we might be onto something.

Sometime in 2010, Jon was down in St. George, Utah, preparing for his Tuacahn show. He had done some teacher workshops in a local store called The Piano Guys and had become friends with the owner, Paul Anderson. Jon went into the piano store that week and asked Paul if he could practice on a piano for his show. Paul had seen the success that Jon's Taylor Swift song had on YouTube, and Paul proposed that they collaborate. He wanted Jon to perform while he (an amateur videographer) filmed and produced piano videos, free of charge, to release on Paul's piano store's YouTube channel, The Piano Guys. Paul envisioned Jon promoting his music while Paul promoted his piano store at the same time. They tried a few of Jon's previously recorded piano tunes together and quickly saw this as a win-win.

And so, Jon, Steve, and Chuck Meyers (a dear friend and producer of Jon's earlier albums) got to work on producing a brand-new tune to be released on The Piano Guys channel. In addition, Jon asked the members on his mailing list to view and share this new video, "Michael Meets Mozart." In this video Jon wanted to discover and highlight all the amazing, innovative ways that Steve was able to produce musical sounds on the cello. Plus, they had seen that the mashing up of two song ideas was something that was really catchy. To our sheer delight, this song went viral also. We began to see not only YouTube views but iTunes purchases. We realized we were indeed onto something promising.

At the same time, Steve had moved to a new area, onto the same street as music producer, songwriter, and recording engineer Al van der Beek. Steve and Al began collaborating musically in Al's home studio, and the two of them brimmed with ideas. That same year, Jon, Steve, Al, and Paul began working on writing songs, filming them, and posting them on YouTube under The Piano Guys channel.

Jon still had lots of performing obligations and was still consumed with producing his annual Christmas show, and all of the guys were working overtime writing, learning, and producing music videos and posting them on the internet. To our surprise, the YouTube channel began to grow at unprecedented speeds, and before we knew it, we had an artist manager from New York City asking to meet with us.

We put him off for months because, honestly, the channel was doing so well without a manager that at this point we didn't see a need for one. But the New York manager was persistent, and we finally agreed to at least meet with him.

At the time of the scheduled meeting, Jon was unable to attend because he was playing somewhere, so I went with Al, Steve, and Paul to meet with David Simone, Winston Simone, and David's wife, Shelley Ross. They were absolutely the most delightful people. David shared with us the names of some of the artists he had managed, and we were blown away at the experience these people had. They were all very persuasive. Shelley even talked to me for a long time after the official meeting to resolve some concerns and help me feel like we could trust them. The thing that was the most convincing to us was that they said we wouldn't be locked into a contract. They wanted to work with us, and if we were happy with what they did, then we could continue to work together. If we weren't happy, we could walk away at any time.

Having a manager was accompanied by the decision to form an official partnership with Steve, Paul, and Al. For Jon and me, this partnership placed us in new territory that we had never navigated before. First of all, it made the most sense that the official voting members in the partnership had to be limited to the four partners, no wives included. That was really hard for us, because Jon and I had worked together as a team on every business decision for the past two decades. All of a sudden, it felt like I had no voice, and, quite frankly, I was a little concerned about this.

But as Jon and I prayed about these decisions, we felt really good about going forward with this partnership. It actually ended up being a relief to be able to turn all of the worry and headache and burden of helping manage Jon's musical career over to someone else. This enabled me to focus on my kids—and believe me, they took everything I had, especially because that year ended up being a pretty rough year with me being diagnosed with breast cancer. Luckily it wasn't very serious, but it was an added trial and hardship, requiring surgery and radiation. So, in that respect, being able to turn everything over to the Guys was a huge blessing.

Once the partnership was officially organized and the other three Guys quit their previous day jobs and focused full time on The Piano Guys channel, it was amazing what they began to accomplish. The knowledge, creativity, ingenuity, and wit that resulted from these Guys' combined efforts were a joy and blessing to be a part of. Just reading comments of how the music inspired, comforted, or brought joy or happiness to people was and is so overwhelming. We realized then, and realize now, the incredible purpose and blessings that have resulted from the gifts and talents and hard work that all of The Piano Guys, with the support of their wives, have brought to the partnership. They have taken this little venture to places that would have been impossible for Jon and me to do alone. We have been able to see the blessings that were given by Jon's dad years earlier come to fruition though The Piano Guys' union.

But here is the embarrassing truth. At first, this partnership was really hard for me. I felt like we had just handed over something we had spent twenty years building up. And those twenty years represented the most heart-wrenching blood, sweat, tears, and faith we had to endure. Even though it felt right to join The Piano Guys' partnership, it was a difficult transition. And then, once we began to share all things equally (which decision came after prayer, analysis, and professional advice, and was determined by all four Guys to be the best way to establish the partnership), I began struggling with something else. It quickly began to feel like the other Guys were experiencing the financial benefits of the growth of the business that Jon and I could not enjoy because we were still trying to dig ourselves out of the effects of our earlier embezzlement. This situation tried me and Jon to the core.

I remember vividly one night in particular when I just lost it. It was the night of Annie's high school graduation. The other three Guys and their wives had gone on a couple of fun trips together in conjunction with some film shoots. We had zero extra money, and I felt that Jon and I should play it safe and keep the money that the business would have allotted for me to go on the trips. After Annie's graduation, as we talked about the situation, I finally exploded. "This is just not fair! I feel as if the other Piano Guys are so quickly benefiting with the help of our career that we worked so long to build, enjoying the fruits of success while we still struggle to make ends meet!"

Jon was silent for a few minutes before saying, "Well, this isn't 'our' career. It never was. Right from the start we tried to consecrate it to the Lord. Remember? From the beginning we have wanted to put our lives and this career in His hands. We have always said that we would be willing to do whatever He asked of us to do, and so now we both feel this is what He is asking us to do."

I sat in silence, absorbing Jon's words. Tears clouded my vision as the realization of this truth penetrated right through me. Yes. I had always said we would only pursue this career as long as the Lord sustained it. Now that it felt like He was asking something in a manner that was really hard for us, did I believe in trusting in the Lord or not? I thought I did. As I reasoned this out in my mind and in my heart, it was as if a light went on inside me, and I was filled with peace. At that moment, any anger and resentment I was struggling with disappeared. I could see more clearly that our situation was not the other Guys' fault. Like us, they were simply seeking God's will in their lives and in this partnership. For this feeling of unity of purpose that I was filled with, I was so thankful. And I was truly happy for them.

Early on in our marriage, Jon found a promise that President Ezra Taft Benson had given to those who would consecrate their lives to the Lord and His purposes:

"Men and women who turn their lives over to God will

find out that he can make a lot more out of their lives than they can. He will deepen their joys, expand their vision, quicken their minds, strengthen their muscles, lift their spirits, multiply their blessings, increase their opportunities, comfort their souls, raise up friends, and pour out peace. Whoever will lose his life in God will find he has eternal life" ("Jesus Christ—Gifts and Expectations," *New Era,* May 1975).

Jon and I clung to this promise as if our lives depended on it. We believed in it. We tried so hard to make it our mantra. Now we were being asked to live it, to truly believe in this promise, and to trust God implicitly.

As I prayerfully sought for help with this matter, I realized I was being proud. I was taking credit for something that wasn't even mine. Had the Lord not given us everything we had ever achieved? The talent. The ideas. The people who helped us. Even the very breath that sustained us from minute to minute. We owed everything to Him. If He wanted to take what we, in our shortsightedness, considered "our career" and use it however He wanted, then who was I to question Him? How crazy would it be to not appreciate the huge benefit and blessing it would bring to our family? Or to not take great joy in the opportunity for so many to feel of God's love through music! Had I really consecrated my all to Him or not? My answer was that I wanted to. I reasoned within myself, "I trust Him. I submit to Him. And I want to do whatever He wants me to." And we definitely felt this was what He wanted us to do. With that realization came the greatest feeling of peace. Therein lay the power to let go of any resentment and emotions of comparison and just put it all in God's hands.

The thing that makes partnerships difficult is the natural

man inside each of us that we seek to overcome. This is also true with our interactions in our families, neighborhoods, communities, and wards. We have to work together and trust each other and consecrate our efforts together to accomplish a greater good. While doing so, each of us is working on an individual journey to overcome jealousy, envy, competition, and pride.

It is an enormous blessing to be united with The Piano Guys in feeling like our lives belong to the Lord and that we are merely stewards over them. It is a huge blessing to be able to have this mentality extend into our business partnership. I have come to this: If we trust in the Lord, we can let Him worry about any discrepancies. This career was not mine. It was not Jon's. It never belonged to us. It was the Lord's, and He could do with it as He pleased.

I once heard a quote that is often attributed to Harry S. Truman, which has helped me so much with my service in the

The Piano Guys, 2015, Red Rocks, Colorado.

Church. It says, "You will be amazed at what you can accomplish in this work, when you don't care who gets the credit." This good advice has helped me so many times beat back my natural-man tendencies, not worry about myself, and just focus on seeking to do the most good. I have a friend who tells her kids when they complain that something isn't fair, "You're right, life isn't fair. And if it was, you'd have a lot less."

As Jon and I threw all our heart and soul behind The Piano Guys' partnership, we discovered a blessing beyond our wildest imaginations. The united efforts of all four Guys, and their incredible wives, has created something light-years beyond what Jon and I could have done on our own. Not to mention all of the ways we have been personally blessed from the rich friendships, faith, and united strength from our union. I truly love them and think of them as brothers and sisters.

Because all four of the partners seek to consecrate their lives and their talents to the Lord, they are in unity, seeking to keep the Spirit in everything they do as a group. This has been such a blessing. It has been great to feel unified when they decide how much to be on the road and away from family, when they seek to choose songs that have good lyrics and videos, even when they turn down performing at events on Sundays. This unity is one reason they have been so blessed to experience some amazing miracles as far as doors opening up to allow them to accomplish different projects.

The Piano Guys' partnership is a testimony to us that President Benson's promises are true. When we turn our lives over to the Lord and trust Him, He will make so much more out of our lives than we are able to do on our own.

The Lord taught, "For whosoever will save his life shall lose it: and whosoever will lose his life for my sake shall find it" (Matthew 16:25). For me, joining with The Piano Guys was one of those tests to see how much I actually trusted the Lord. Was I willing to give up something that I felt such an ownership over? Was I willing to trust the Lord? Yes. I was willing, and time and time again I've realized that the Lord always has my back. He always blesses me way beyond what would have happened if I had followed my own plan. Sometimes His way is a hard road. Sometimes it takes me through paths that are painful. But every single time, when I look back, I'm always so grateful for what I've learned and who it has helped me to become.

I truly believe that the tutorial we underwent in learning to trust God in building a career helped me to face each day that I woke up and didn't know where Annie was. I would repeat in my mind Job's words, "The Lord gave, and the Lord hath taken away; blessed be the name of the Lord" (Job 1:21). And I tried really hard to mean it. I can now see how trusting God's timing with Jon's career was essential to allowing our faith in Him and His plan for us to come to fruition. That faith, though it was harder than anything I had ever done before, played a role in helping me believe we would find Annie when and if God wanted us to.

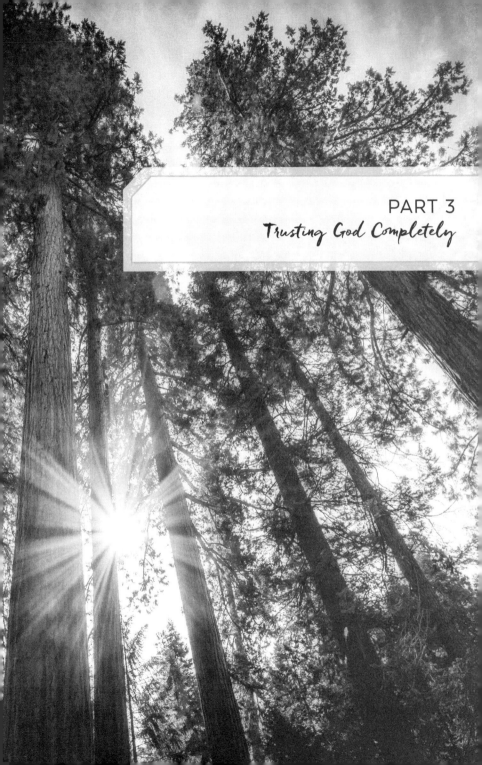

PART 3
Trusting God Completely

CHAPTER 8

Bound by Covenants

Monday, October 24, 2016

As I left the search to go to the airport, returned my rental car, and went to my gate, going through the motions of doing responsible things, my mind and heart felt as if they were in another dimension. I was leaving Oregon, and my daughter was lost somewhere on a mountain. Everyone and everything around me felt hazy and unreal. I didn't feel real.

My number-one concern right then was to write to my twins on their missions. I was so concerned about them and how they were doing after hearing the news that their sister was missing. Chris's mission president had let us have a brief conversation with him, and it was reassuring to hear his voice and to feel that he was handling it well, being sustained through the Spirit. But Jonny's mission president did not want us to talk to Jonny until we had some further information to give him. Not knowing how Jonny was doing made me extremely worried.

I sat down at the gate and pulled out my phone to write to my boys. Where to even begin? What was I supposed to say? I prayed and asked the Lord to help me to be able to comfort my boys who were an ocean away. My sweet, sweet boys, who loved their sister beyond description. My heart hurt for them, especially since they were in a foreign country and had been there only a few weeks. They were still homesick and trying to adjust to missionary life. How would they handle something so traumatic? What could I possibly share that would give them comfort and assurance?

And then the answer came. "Covenants. Speak to them about your covenants."

Though our family was in disarray and we were separated and scattered—one child in England, one in Ireland, and one

Jonny, Annie, and Chris overlooking Salt Lake City, Utah.

most likely in the spirit world—I had something of great power and comfort to give them: my testimony of the binding blessings of our covenants. Those covenants would keep us bound together now and throughout eternity. We could feel complete and absolute peace with that knowledge. Despite anything that we might suffer in this life, our binding covenants, if we were faithful to them, would guarantee our ultimate victory, happiness, and reunion. Even now, I have never felt more thankful for my covenants in my life.

So I wrote to my twins about the details of going to meet Annie, her not being at her apartment, the last time I spoke to her, the search and rescue, and a little of the nightmare we had been living the last few days:

> *When we first discovered Annie's disappearance, I was faced with some pretty horrible possibilities of what might have happened to her. As Dad and I talked about it, every possible scenario was horrific. But I testify that the thing that gave us strength was the knowledge of our covenants, which are cords that bind us to God and Him to us. As I thought of these covenants I felt power to be able to access the powers of the priesthood concerning Annie. I was able, with surety, to ask God to hear my words as I made my requests known unto Him. The cries I offered to the Lord that night were more than desperate pleas for help, they were more an act of exercising faith and power in Annie's behalf.*

Then I explained more about the search and who came and helped and what it had been like, because I knew they would want to know every detail.

But we have not found her. I'm flying home to Sarah today, even though most of our family and friends are staying to try and find Annie. There really is no hope that she's still alive, but we so want to find her body.

Personally, I feel so comforted thinking of her having passed and being safe and loved and warm. I know she knows how much we love her. I believe she knows and feels how much we love her even stronger in the spirit world than we were ever able to express here. And I know she knows how much you guys love her.

I take great comfort in knowing Heavenly Father and Jesus Christ have enfolded her in Their arms, especially because she loved Them so much. Even though she wasn't perfect, she always tried with all of her heart to love and follow Jesus Christ.

I hope this has not been too hard for you boys. So, remember, we have our covenants. We are safe in these bonds. Our family is bound together for eternity.

. . . I hope while you guys are on your missions, just like Dad did when he lost his sister while on his mission, that you will have an extra support and closeness to the Spirit which will bring you comfort and solace. I pray this may be so.

At one point during all of this, Dad, Spencer, and I reiterated our absolute knowledge of the witnesses we have received of the reality of God, His Son, and Their plan of salvation. Your service right now is to bring these truths to anyone who will listen, so that as many as will, may have these same blessings of knowledge, peace, strength, and comfort with whatever life brings. And most importantly, we need to help people to make covenants which bind them to God. These covenants are essential to our full joy.

. . . I love you both so much, with every fiber of my being. I love you.

Mom

Upon landing I received their responses, and they brought so much comfort and assurance. The following is part of Jonny's letter written the same day, Monday, October 24, 2016:

Family, can you even believe or comprehend this week? I can't. Wow. Surely this is a time of most trial and mourning. But it is ok to mourn and weep and cry and be sad. Let us, Mom, for it is a gift, even. But let us know in whom we trust.

I was so, so, so comforted by your email, Mom. . . . I was in Athlone with my companion when we got the call from President. I was a little nervous at first, especially as President started out the conversation by saying, "I have some grievous news to tell you . . . about your sister, Annie."

Immediately I prepared myself for the worst, hoping that she was just sick or something, but he proceeded. "Annie has been lost for six days. She went off hiking last Sunday and hasn't come back. No one has heard from her, and that is all they know at the moment." My heart and mind and emotions didn't even know what to do. I didn't comprehend it quite fully.

. . . I started to fade emotionally. I immediately began to think about all of the memories I've made with Annie. The countless number of amazing memories. Of her driving me

and my friends anywhere and everywhere, of her selfless high school life she gave to serving her two younger brothers to make their teenage years the best experience possible. Driving us down to Orem, driving us to Denny's, everything started coming to my mind. The amount of influence she's had on my life. All the ways she has shaped and formed who I am today. And I, Jonny, started to get really, really, sad, even to the point of tears.

. . . I told my companion "Let's try and catch an earlier bus home, please." So, we went and checked, but there wasn't an earlier bus. At this point I was faced with two options: 1- sit and wait an hour and a half for the next bus, and let myself take in and think about what I've been told and try to find peace of mind, or, 2- go out and tract, and try to bring souls to Christ.

Never in my life, and my whole missionary experience (and hopefully for the rest of it,) will I ever have a better excuse or reason to "take a break" or "relax and not find." But the Spirit pressed upon my soul, and I didn't take a break or relax. In that moment, I chose to show, not just the Lord something, but myself something. And that something was my true and pure desire to do His work and build His kingdom. Never have I had a more powerful experience tracting in my entire life.

. . . I testified to an old woman that I know we can live with our families forever. I know it! As I was thinking of my dear sister at the time, what power came, immense power came, and I have never testified with that strong of a spirit in my life. Absolutely amazing, and my testimony is

forever deepened. Strengthened. Expanded. Magnified. Real. Sincere.

It was a most wonderful experience, and I was able to show the Lord my desire to bring His children to the truth, by putting forth effort when it was by far the most difficult, and I know I will be blessed for it. Nothing can stay this work, for it is true, and I can't deny it.

. . . This morning I knew I would be writing to you guys. And so, I sat down, and for the first time I really thought about you all, thought about everything. And I just bawled and bawled and bawled. I wept earlier in the week over Annie and found comfort in weeping. But I wept this morning because of you, Mom.

I tried to imagine what you might be feeling, a dear mother, who has just lost her little girl, literally lost her, and I absolutely wept, for a good half hour. . . . It makes me think of Annie and how much we love her, and I thought of you Dad, and Spencer, and Sarah, and I still weep while writing this, for my mind has started to finally take all of it in.

Mom, my love for you is so, so strong, and I want you to know that I have turned every single prayer towards you being strengthened. I want to ease all of your fears and worries, especially yours, Mom, and let you know how I am doing with all of this craziness. I am doing absolutely amazing! So, so, so good. Of course, I am sad, but I have found peace in the Savior, and through talking to Him, I have been uplifted and strengthened throughout the week.

But never, till this morning, did I realize how serious and how hard to bear this past week must have been for all of you. Personally . . . I am comforted, and I know with a surety that we are going to not just see Annie again, but we will live with her forever. The Lord has truly given me the perspective I need and seek, and it is amazing. We can be comforted and know that Annie is our dear sister, and that we will be with her again, and how sweet will be our joy when we are again united with her.

I have a firm faith that the Lord can work miracles and that she could still be alive and found. If so, may we rejoice. But let us not let the outcome affect our faith.

. . . When I first found out and started praying for Annie, my immediate prayers were, "I have faith that you can find her and help her. Please bless her to be found and to be safe." My prayers were all centered around Annie being found.

But as I continued to pray throughout the week, the Spirit guided my prayers to be more like this, "Lord, I know that Thou canst do all things, and according to our faith you work among us. Bless me to be comforted with whatever outcome, and help me to be able to accept and to only desire Thy will to be brought forth in this situation. If it is Thy will that she go, help me to have peace in it and gain the faith to be happy with it." Now that is a good prayer.

. . . Praying this kind of prayer gave me comfort. For I know that whatever happens with little Annie will be the Lord's will, and I can be happy about that because of the faith I have in Him and this gospel.

. . . Don't get me wrong in any way. Losing Annie is horrific, and I'm not Mister Jolly Cakes over here, bouncing off the walls. I am deeply sad, and I weep, because I will miss

not being with Annie for the rest of my mortal life, and I absolutely adore the memories I've made with her.

But, at the center of my soul I rejoice and am overly filled with joy. For I know in whom I have trusted. And upon the rock am I built. Yea, and whosoever buildeth upon this rock, shall not fall.

If you haven't already, Fam, find this joy. Find this amazing most sweet joy that the Lord is willing to bless us with in this moment of trial. He will lift your spirits and help you back up. I trust you have already done this. He stands supreme.

As I've thought of you, Family and Mom, I wrote, "The depth of the Atonement is amazing. Every tear that is shed, every single one that comes out of your eye, Mom, over our dearest sister, came out of Jesus' eyes too. That is just absolutely amazing. Amazing and beautiful and extremely hard to comprehend."

As I sought for understanding this morning, I was able to comprehend this to a greater degree. And boy did it bring strength and power. If you are suffering, and perhaps even feeling a little bitter toward God, try to comprehend this, and His Atonement. Pray for help, because losing Annie is a great chance to understand the Atonement greater. I know that it's so hard to do this with such an extreme trial placed before you. But, try, Mom and Dad. Try to think of this as a chance to better understand Him, and what He went through, and your joy will be full. I promise you that. Just think of what God went through, sending His Only Begotten Son down here, to experience far worse than we could imagine. Could you imagine what it would be like, as a parent, to watch your child suffer and die for the sins of the world? I can't. But let it strengthen us.

You will weep, and you will be sad and mourn for many days, months, and even years, but your joy will be full, and your love will be fuller than ever before. You will weep for how great a loss, but joy will be at the center of your soul because you trust in Him.

It's weird to think that the two can go together. But this morning I experienced the two emotions. I was sad, bawling, sobbing. But, while I listened to "I Believe in Christ," instead of sobbing in bitterness, I sobbed for joy. Because, we do believe in Christ, and He does stand supreme. So, come what may, truly come what may, (you say it all the time, Dad), and love it.

. . . I want you guys to know how much love and support you have received from the missionaries and people here in Ireland and Scotland. All the Ireland Dublin Zone missionaries took a day to fast together, and pray every single night. That's over forty different missionaries fasting an extra day when they were all out working hard and very hungry, all for someone they don't know. Amazing.

The Mullingar Branch had a branch fast and prayed every single night. I don't even know half of these members, and they especially don't know my sister. Yet, they have all fasted. Amazing.

The countless number of members and nonmembers praying all around the world. I heard from the members that Annie's story was in the papers all the way over here, and that's how they all found out about it. It has gone worldwide.

To all the people back home, family, friends, hundreds in Oregon helping, all of the prayers, thank you. There are so many, and the amount of support absolutely blows me away. It is a testimony to me of this church, and that it is led by a loving God.

I want you to know that your prayers have saved me, and that I feel more love towards you guys than you can ever know. Being out here on the mission, I feel pretty much helpless in finding my sister. And if any of you know me, you know I would be the first one to get to Oregon, searching without sleep, night and day, more diligently than anyone, besides maybe my dad, until I found my dear sister. . . . So, you guys helping and praying has really helped me feel better and brought me so much peace. Thank you. I can't thank you enough.

I love you all so much,
Elder Jonny Schmidt

Chris's letter, received Monday, October 24, 2016:

. . . I have felt like the Lord has just picked me up off the ground and squeezed me, not letting me come back down. I have felt so much comfort it's insane. But I know right where it comes from. It comes from God, and it's because all of you have been praying and fasting. I can't believe the way that I have felt these past few days, "For I will go before your face. I will be on your right hand and on your left, and my Spirit shall be in your hearts, and mine angels round about you, to bear you up" (Doctrine and Covenants 84:88). Seriously, I have felt like this. And I have so much joy and am so grateful.

My testimony of God's plan of happiness has grown so much. I am really grateful for the example Christ set and the comfort He gives me. I love the fact that I can be out here, being a guide for people to find this in their own lives. It is so humbling and amazing. And not to mention, it heals my soul. I don't know what I would be like if I didn't have this ideal setting of being on a mission, to rely on the Lord completely. If I didn't have the opportunity to see people change their lives to be closer to God. If I didn't have so much love and prayers back at home. I praise God with all my heart because of His hand in our lives. His plan for us to grow, how He comforts us in our afflictions, and how these trials make us grow closer to Him. There is only one place to turn when something like this happens, and that is to Christ, with your whole heart. Grieving in humble prayer. Grateful that all things will work together for our good, and overwhelmed at the love that is there, and is real.

I have been walking with angels these past few days, and I mean it. I pray that we turn our hearts and all our pain to Christ. And our bitter cup He will fill with sweet.

I caught a sickness at the same time I heard the news of sweet Annie. It was interesting, because my body and my soul were damaged at the same time. As I spent time healing my body it felt like an inward effort. I had to pay attention to myself, and I had to do things for me. But to heal the soul, turning inward doesn't work. The triage of the soul is found in turning outward.

So, I went out and taught lessons, served, comforted others, and loved these people. And that is what has healed my soul. The Savior didn't just redeem our souls at the time He suffered for us in the flesh. But He can and continues to redeem our souls every time they are hurt here on this earth.

. . . On Saturday our whole mission had the opportunity to hear from five General Authorities and their wives for two hours. I was sitting front and center, and the highlight was the end speaker, President Russell M. Nelson. He spoke, and we made eye contact plenty of times. The Spirit was so strong in that chapel, that my throat was sore from having a lump in it the whole time.

President Nelson was about to close, and then he paused, and said, "I sense that some of you are worried about your families." And he looked right at me. Then he said, "Turn to Doctrine and Covenants, section 31." We turned there and he told us to replace our name with Thomas's name.

"[Chris], my son, blessed are you because of your faith in my work.

"Behold, you have had many afflictions because of your family; nevertheless, I will bless you and your family. . . .

"Lift up your heart and rejoice, for the hour of your mission is come; and your tongue shall be loosed, and you shall declare glad tidings of great joy unto this generation.

"You shall declare the things which have been revealed to my servant, Joseph Smith, Jun. You shall begin to preach from this time forth, yea, to reap in the field which is white already to be burned.

"Therefore, thrust in your sickle with all your soul, and your sins are forgiven you, and you shall be laden with sheaves upon your back, for the laborer is worthy of his hire. Wherefore, your family shall live."

President Nelson paused here and said something along

the lines of, whether it is in the flesh and bone they live, or in the presence of God, they will live.

"Behold, verily I say unto you, go from them only for a little time, and declare my word, and I will prepare a place for them.

"Yea, I will open the hearts of the people, and they will receive you. . . .

"Be faithful unto the end, and lo, I am with you. These words are not of man nor of men, but of me, even Jesus Christ, your Redeemer, by the will of the Father. Amen."

And then President Nelson . . . made the passage of scripture an apostolic promise to those who were worried about their families. And he said that staying in the mission was the very best thing we can do for our families.

Halfway through President Nelson reading the scriptural passage, I bowed my head and cried and cried. And when I looked up he was looking at me like his words were just for me.

I don't know what he knows about me. But I know he's an apostle of the Lord, and I know the Lord knows everything about me. And He knows everything about all of us and what we are going through.

I love you all,
Elder Chris Schmidt

As a mother, I can't even begin to describe how comforting these letters from my boys were. They were okay. They were being sustained and comforted by the Spirit. And they had the peace that comes from understanding that they were safe in the arms of their Savior. Knowing that my boys had this knowledge gave me even greater strength to handle the intense pressure and stress of looking for our lost daughter.

But what enables someone to have such knowledge? From where does such strength and assurance come? For us, it was a by-product of the covenants that we have made with our Heavenly Father and His Son, Jesus Christ.

In my opinion, chapter 53 of Isaiah is one of the most beautiful yet heartbreaking chapters in all of scripture. It explains in part our relationship with God and the covenants we make with Him through Christ. Isaiah describes the sufferings and mission of Jesus Christ:

"He is despised and rejected of men; a man of sorrows, and acquainted with grief: . . . Surely he hath borne our griefs, and carried our sorrows: . . . he was wounded for our transgressions, he was bruised for our iniquities: the chastisement of our peace was upon him; and with his stripes we are healed. All we like sheep have gone astray; we have turned every one to his own way; and the Lord hath laid on him the iniquity of us all. . . . Yet it pleased the Lord to bruise him; he hath put him to grief: when thou shalt make his soul an offering for sin, he shall see his seed" (Isaiah 53:3–6, 10).

What does it mean that the Lord shall see His seed? Who is His seed? I believe that it is anyone who loves the Lord and seeks to follow Him. Anyone. From any religion. All good people, all over the world. Maybe they don't even know about Jesus Christ, but if they are seeking goodness and virtue and truth during their lifetimes, then I believe they are His seed. Because every good thing comes from Christ.

One of the ways we become Christ's seed is to make covenants. The first covenant we make that binds us to God is the baptismal covenant. We promise to take His name upon us and to follow Him, and He in turn promises us to give us His Holy Spirit to help and guide us in our life's pursuit of following Him.

Baptism is just the beginning of the covenants we can make with God. Through the Prophet Joseph Smith, the priesthood was restored, with the authority to administer further covenants. With these further covenants, or promises, that we make to God, even more blessings and power come from God to us.

The very good news and tidings of great joy are that there is more. There is more joy and peace and assurance to be had through making covenants with Christ. We can be tied more tightly and intimately to Him. We can have more help and power, beyond our own, to overcome weakness, face

Our family, August 2016.

challenges, and taste of the fruits of love. The ancient prophet King Benjamin explained it so well in the Book of Mormon. He said:

"And now, because of the covenant which ye have made ye shall be called the children of Christ, his sons, and his daughters; for behold, this day he hath spiritually begotten you; for ye say that your hearts are changed through faith on his name; therefore, ye are born of him and have become his sons and his daughters.

"And under this head ye are made free, and there is no other head whereby ye can be made free. There is no other name given whereby salvation cometh; therefore, I would that ye should take upon you the name of Christ, all you that have entered into the covenant with God that ye should be obedient unto the end of your lives.

"And it shall come to pass that whosoever doeth this . . . shall know the name by which he is called; for he shall be called by the name of Christ" (Mosiah 5:7–9).

This is why we send our children out into the world to publish this message of joy and peace to anyone willing to listen.

I know, and have felt without doubt, the power of these covenants in my life, especially as I sat at the airport thinking about what I could write my boys to comfort them at the loss of their sister. I am so grateful for the power I feel now and felt then from my covenants.

CHAPTER 9

The Power of Covenants

During the Christmastime of 2004, I had taken my then three-year-old, Sarah, shopping to pick up one last gift I had forgotten to get. It was just a day or two before Christmas and absolutely the worst time of all to go to the mall, but I had to get this last gift.

The store was packed. It was a nightmare, and I chided myself for coming into such a crowded situation, like Disneyland in July. We finally found the item and made our way to the counter. As I finished my transaction, I turned around, and—you guessed it, Sarah was missing. I'm sure this has happened to the majority of moms at some point in their child-raising careers. Whether your child is missing for a few seconds or several minutes, every second is filled with an intense desire to get that child back into your arms.

I began looking all around for Sarah and calling her name.

I don't alarm easily, but as the minutes went on and I couldn't see her anywhere, I became more and more anxious. There were just so many people.

I looked through clothing rounders and all over every inch of the store that I could see, but still I couldn't find her. Horrible thoughts began to enter my mind, and I began to feel panic. I had been praying silently the entire time, but suddenly I had the thought to draw upon more power.

So I stood still amidst a sea of people and silently called upon priesthood power, through the temple covenants I had made, that not a hair of Sarah's head would be touched and that she wouldn't be injured in any way until I had her back safely.

As I did this, a surge of energy and power flowed through my body, from my head to my toes. With it came an absolute assurance that Sarah would be unequivocally safe, and with that knowledge also came the thought that she was hiding in a clothing rounder. I then calmly looked through the rounders until I found her.

This experience was somewhat of a shock to me because I had never thought to call upon power through my priesthood covenants before. No one had taught me to do so. I had heard of early pioneer women healing through their faith. And, as I related earlier, I had experienced pleading for healing for my baby Chris through faith. But those experiences seemed different from what I had just experienced with the power I felt I had accessed through my covenants. As I thought of my temple priesthood covenants, I felt a literal power course through me to bring me peace and help me know what to do. If you think about it, when we make covenants in the temple, one of the ultimate covenants we make arms our children with protection and power.

Elder M. Russell Ballard gave a wonderful talk in which he explained the power available to women through their priesthood covenants. He said:

"When men and women go to the temple, they are both endowed with the same . . . priesthood power. While the authority of the priesthood is directed through priesthood keys, and priesthood keys are held only by worthy men, access to the power and blessings of the priesthood is available to all of God's children.

"As President Joseph Fielding Smith explained: 'The blessings of the priesthood are not confined to men alone. These blessings are also poured out upon . . . all the faithful women of the Church. . . . ' ["Magnifying Our Callings in the Priesthood," *Improvement Era,* June 1970].

"Those who have . . . received their endowment in the house of the Lord are eligible for rich and wonderful blessings. The endowment is literally a gift of power. All who enter the house of the Lord officiate in the ordinances of the priesthood.

"Our Father in Heaven is generous with His power. All men and all women have access to this power for help in their lives. All who have made sacred covenants with the Lord and who honor those covenants are eligible . . . to receive the fulness of the gospel, and, ultimately, to become heirs alongside Jesus Christ of all our Father has" ("Men and Women and Priesthood Power," *Ensign,* September 2014).

This teaching from an Apostle of the Lord was such a great explanation to me of what I had experienced when calling down protection and power in behalf of my lost daughter.

How could I have had any idea at the time that this experience was just a type of a similar experience I would have when Annie disappeared, but of a much greater magnitude? Elder Ballard's talk not only explains some of the blessings of our priesthood covenants to women, but it also is a testament of the role women have in the Church.

Let me share another experience that taught me the importance of the power we can receive from our covenants.

In the fall of 1998 I had been struggling with feelings of worthlessness. More than just feeling worthless, I felt like I had lost my personality. I felt broken down. I felt weak, insecure, and emotional. While trying to continue to care for my children and their demanding routines, inside I was wasting away.

One of the last times I had felt like this—emotionally, spiritually, and physically wasted—was on my mission to Norway in 1989. After being on my feet all day from knocking door to door, day after day, my back couldn't hold up my body anymore, and my ribs began to dislocate. And, yet, I had this conflicting voice of guilt in my head saying, "Don't be a wimp and get to work. Work. Work!"

When I finally hobbled off the plane and came home, I came home a different person. I felt weak and vulnerable. That was the best thing that could have happened to me, because it gave me a greater perspective and a desire to live a life of service to the Lord. I prayed and pled with the Lord to help my body heal and help me put my life back together. As a result, my commitment and dedication to His work became a part of my soul.

The breakdown I experienced in 1998 had slowly occurred over a year and a half. I felt like my body had been physically destroyed from carrying the twins full-term. Emotionally, I was completely worn out. Trying to meet the emotional needs of so many little ones had left me totally empty.

Sometimes I had to turn off my emotions and just go through the motions without feeling, because I had nothing left to give. Spiritually, it was the hardest. There just wasn't any quiet time to ponder. I was in a spiritual desert.

My prayers, though I offered them daily, were not ones of quiet communication and a desire to serve selflessly, but rather cries for help. "Help me! Please, help me. Please help me get through this. Please help my children. I need to be healed. I need to be healed emotionally, physically, and spiritually." It humbled me to the dust, and I felt weak and vulnerable to the point of breaking.

One night when I was feeling this way, Jon and I went to the temple. I don't know if there is any way to adequately explain what I felt, but as we took our seats for the session, two young girls sat next to me. I could tell they were both newlyweds, full of life and energy. As I looked at them, I thought to myself, "You have no idea the thrashing that is ahead of you. You poor things. You have no idea!"

But then, as I sat through the session and thought of my efforts that past year, I began to feel love and acceptance from the Lord. I began to think of extremely draining parenting challenges I had experienced over the year—including almost losing Chris—and again, I felt an accompanying feeling of love and approval from the Lord.

And then the endowment focused on sacrificing, even as our Savior taught us to sacrifice through the example of His life, and I suddenly experienced a flowing energy and power and healing that washed throughout my body to such a degree that I felt completely overcome. The words came into my mind, "I accept your offering of sacrifice." A continual flood of warmth and love and approval portrayed to my mind and heart the words over and over again, "Good job. Good job. Good job."

As I renewed my covenant to sacrifice all that I had and all that I was, the feelings of warmth and love and healing intensified to a degree that tears flowed. It seemed as if time stood still, and the Spirit taught my spirit things I had known intellectually but was then feeling so deeply, spiritually, that they seemed like priceless spiritual treasures.

I realized that all of my sacrifices, as overwhelming as they were, were only a similitude of the sacrifice of the Savior. My appreciation for the Savior and His Atonement were magnified and deepened. It cannot be described in words; it can only be experienced through the Spirit. We can't really appreciate the law of sacrifice until we have truly sacrificed.

And then the Lord revealed to my mind that it was all worth it, that it was a righteous endeavor I had endured through. The feelings I experienced were sweet, pure, intense feelings of approval and acceptance and love. I knew that my efforts had been sealed by the Holy Ghost. I knew that this would be similar to how it would feel at the end of our lives, when we would stand before the Lord. We will feel a sweet and consuming feeling of love and approval, and we will be sealed up unto everlasting life.

I cannot sufficiently express my gratitude for this sweet experience. Needless to say, I felt healed and whole. I felt renewed and filled with hope and energy and joy.

And then I looked at the two young girls next to me, and I prayed for them that they would be strengthened in their personal life journeys, and that they both would be blessed to come to know the Lord and to feel of His love and help as they fulfilled their individual missions on this earth. I felt so much love for these two girls, there wasn't anything I wouldn't do to help them in any way I could. The last year and a half of struggling in motherhood and wondering about my worth as a woman was all worth it. Every last bit of it.

Even when I headed into a very hectic day the next day, including rushing Chris to an urgent care facility with bad ear infections, the feelings I felt in the temple stayed with me. I didn't feel like a broken and empty woman. I felt like a woman of promise, a woman who had chosen to follow a path that would help her become more like the Savior. I was filled with a renewed energy to fulfill my responsibilities with power and might. I was filled with a greater desire to serve my Lord and fulfill His purposes for me in this life. The promise of Isaiah had literally come to pass for me:

"He shall feed his flock like a shepherd: he shall gather the lambs with his arm, and carry them in his bosom, and shall gently lead those that are with young. . . .

"He giveth power to the faint; and to them that have no might he increaseth strength.

"Even the youths shall faint and be weary, and the young men shall utterly fall:

"But they that wait upon the Lord shall renew their strength; they shall mount up with wings as eagles; they shall run, and not be weary; and they shall walk, and not faint" (Isaiah 40:11, 29–31.)

These are the blessings of the temple and of the covenants that we make therein. They are priceless. They are precious. They are of such worth to our lives that they are worth every effort to seek to attain them. They are the source of strength and power we need when hard trials come upon us.

CHAPTER 10

Finding Annie

November 2016

When I arrived home from Oregon, Sarah ran into my arms. We stood in the kitchen and cried and cried and cried. Friends and ward members had literally filled every room in our home with flowers and notes of condolences. Such acts of kindness and expressions of love sustained and carried us through this trial. Notes of sympathy and strength continued to arrive for us, and we were overwhelmed with the support that we felt.

One letter that I'll never forget came from a little boy who drew a picture of a mountain. On his picture there was a path leading out of the mountain and an arrow pointing the way "out." At the bottom of the page he wrote, "Could you please give this to Annie?"

Over the next week Jon and Spencer and our friends and family left the search and came home. Jon really felt that the

Flowers from neighbors and friends line our driveway.

search had covered all accessible areas and that Annie was in a place that was far from the trails. We felt that dogs or expert climbers were needed. Jon was also worried so many people were missing work and leaving their own families on our behalf and would have stayed if we had stayed.

But our daughter was still missing, and we just didn't know what to do next. We had numerous organizations and individuals contact us about what we should do. Every day, Jon spent hours on the phone talking to people, trying to figure out what our best avenues were that we should pursue to find our daughter. It was extremely overwhelming, especially in the exhausted and numb state we were in. Trying to plan, organize, and execute a private search effort was a weight that literally felt crushing.

John Harding was an absolute God-sent angel in our life at this time. For reasons beyond our understanding, John felt compelled to continue in the efforts to search for Annie until she was found. Spencer had asked John to take over after the official search and rescue effort was called off, but the fact that

John actually did take over, and was still committed, was beyond our ability to comprehend. This daunting task of taking the lead to search for our daughter was not just something that he was able to do in his free, retired time—he worked as an executive of a company and had a family with children still at home. Yet he willingly sacrificed so much to help us.

Why? Why would anyone do this for someone else? John said he felt called to do it. But I do not feel like I can ever adequately appreciate this gift of John Harding given to us by a loving Heavenly Father. Maybe it was because there were so many people praying on our behalf. Maybe it was the combined faith of so many that brought down the powers of heaven to bless us with someone to help us to such a degree. All I know is that I'll be forever grateful for the leadership, perseverance, and strength that we received from John Harding.

We spoke with John on the phone for hours, analyzing what we knew, discussing what we still wanted to pursue, and more than anything discussing the implications of what we were experiencing and expressing our faith and trust in the Lord.

John and a few others went back up to search after coming home for a few days of rest. After he had spent the day bushwhacking in remote areas along the Columbia River Gorge, he would talk to us at night, saying things like, "Now, when we find Annie tomorrow, what are your wishes concerning her body?" John's faith was absolutely beyond my ability to understand. He was a calm, faith-filled voice each day amid a tumultuous onslaught of uncertainty, fear, weariness, and sorrow.

We felt like we had not searched the water adequately, and

so we pushed for the river to be dragged. The official search and rescue unit had gone out and done some searching, but for some reason I just felt like we hadn't looked long and hard enough yet. So John Harding and other kind volunteers went out one day to search the river in the gorge across from where Annie's car had been parked.

Third from the left, John Harding, with a group of kind volunteer searchers.

They rented scuba gear and went off on their own, scuba diving the Columbia Gorge. And they almost got arrested because, unbeknownst to any of us, the locks along the gorge are actually considered "ports of entry" into the United States, and therefore are under jurisdiction of Homeland Security. In addition, the places they were searching around the locks were extremely dangerous. If the locks had been opened at any time during their scuba diving, they would have been killed. Luckily, that didn't happen, and the water officers were very understanding as to why they were out on the lake and let them go without arresting them. But it was a very serious matter of which we were completely ignorant. For an anxious mom, waiting at home for the results of the find for the day, it was discouraging and disappointing that their searching was fruitless.

During the first week of November I was particularly distraught, as everything we were trying seemed to be futile. It was hard to keep our faith alive and strong, believing that Heavenly Father was hearing our cries for help. We knew we could rely on our faith with complete assurance, given our past experiences when God had delivered us time and time again. We knew He had the ability to lead us right to Annie. We came to the conclusion that if God wouldn't lead us to Annie, then there had to be a purpose in it that we didn't understand at the time. We had to remind ourselves over and over again of the "but if not" principle.

The "but if not" attitude means that we surrender our own desires to whatever the Lord's will may be. I wanted to find my daughter so badly, but I had to be willing to submit to the fact that our finding Annie may not be the Lord's will. I had to be okay with that because, if my will was not aligned with His, then I would be distancing myself from Him and doing this alone. And on my own I would be a total wreck. He is my all. He is my rock, my foundation, my strength, my support, my Savior, my advocate, and my friend. There is no way I could risk separating myself from Him, especially at such a crucial time as Annie's passing. I'm not smart enough to handle this world on my own. I have and had no choice but to trust Him with absolutely everything—even if it meant not finding my daughter. Still, I was so, so sad that we weren't finding Annie.

It is difficult to describe the anguish of soul I experienced.

My heart was broken with sorrow, yet my grieving was put on hold by the fact that we were consumed with trying to find Annie. As much as my heart ached, I was in a state of pushing forward with all my might and determination to try to find her, while at the same time trying to be willing to submit my will to the Lord's.

When I was wrestling within myself with these emotions, a friend called and said she needed to come by and give me something. She stopped by late Wednesday night, November 2, and brought me two huge scrapbooks filled with stories and memories of Annie. She had sent out Facebook messages, asking people to send any photos or memories they had of Annie. Then this friend and some others spent hours and hours putting together these two giant books for me. They are absolutely priceless. The pictures of Annie, many of which I had never seen, and the stories and memories have become so special to me.

As my friend delivered these gifts, she said, "I have no idea why I needed to bring these over to you today. But I felt Annie pushing me to have these books delivered to you by today. We received so much more material than we ever imagined we would, and the project of putting it all together became more and more overwhelming as more and more stuff arrived. But we have been working around the clock because I felt like Annie wanted you to have these books today."

I bowed my head and tears streamed down my cheeks as I told this friend, "Today is my birthday." My daughter, through dear friends, was reaching out to me in a very real way.

This friend included the following note with the scrapbooks she gave me on my birthday.

Dear Michelle,

I've thought often of our conversation after your return from Oregon, as to why it sometimes takes a tragedy, or a hardship, or loss to express our love and appreciation to one another. As I received hundreds of emails putting these books together this week, I was so touched by one common theme— Annie's love for others. She needed no reason, no excuse, she loved freely and unselfishly, and gifted that love to others. Despite her own personal hardships and battles, she reached out to others who needed her love.

I've a framed quote in my home that I pass by every day, which reads, "Be kind. For everyone you meet is fighting a hard battle." Annie lived her life this way every day.

This past Sunday, it was a blessing to have so many of Annie's friends in my home, working on this book to give to your family. There were tears and laughter and memories shared. Despite all the memories and emails and photos that were shared by so many, I went to bed that evening feeling so troubled. I stayed up much of the night feeling like there was something I was missing that needed to be in the book.

Usually when I can't sleep, I often listen to music or read until my eyes finally succumb to sleep. That evening, I found myself mindlessly humming a song. I woke up the next morning and began again to work on the book, putting pages in the sleeves. Sweet Gretchen offered to come over to help me that day. Again, I was troubled, almost to the point of obsessiveness, that I was missing something.

As we sat and worked on the book together, I began to hum a song. I'm not certain how long I had been humming the song when the words started to come. . . .

. . . As the words came . . . I sang them aloud. I turned to Gretchen and we both wept. I wish I could adequately describe to you the tender feelings and strong presence that we both felt at that moment as I said aloud, "Okay, Annie, okay. Is this what you wanted?"

I immediately did a search to find a song with the words or title "Love You Forever." But to my disappointment, nothing matched the words that popped up on the search.

I went back into the room where Gretchen was working and looked down at the book to see in front of me, a photo of Annie singing as a young girl, at [a school function]. I looked further and saw the caption read, "Jon made a guest appearance, and then Annie came up and sang 'I Will' by the Beatles."

Again, we wept as chills of certainty that this was what Annie wanted, covered our bodies. We searched the song "I Will," from Jon's album, and found the arrangement he wrote, and listened to Annie's beautiful child voice sing [the words.]. . .

Because of the tender experience of discovering Annie singing "I Will," I now know that this book isn't just about the love others have for her, rather it is also Annie's gift of love to you. Annie's life has blessed the life of countless others.

I was so touched by your words online when you said, "Annie would say, 'Love each other. Reach out of your circles and comfort zones and open your heart and minds to those around you. God loves you. Love each other.'" . . .

I will.

Jon accompanying Annie at a school event.

I could feel the love of Annie and the love of the Lord from this experience of receiving these scrapbooks and the details of how they came to be. It strengthened me in such a way that I continued to feel sustained and carried through all of November. This help is what enabled me to get up each morning and push forward through the day—this, along with the prayers of hundreds of thousands of others. Looking back on this experience, I'm still so grateful for this sacred gift.

Meanwhile, we continued to counsel together with John Harding every day. But both Jon and I were kind of living in a fog and were actually really ignorant of so much of what was going on concerning the search for Annie.

I was with some friends one night, and they mentioned something about a website called "Finding Annie Schmidt," which I knew nothing about. I realized I was completely oblivious about who was involved in the search for Annie, what types of efforts were going on, and who was doing what. I needed to force myself out of hiding and get to the bottom of what was going on.

The next day we began researching who had started what websites, who the administrators for the sites were, what conversations were being had, and what organizations were doing what.

We discovered that Jon's cousin, under the direction of my brother, had begun the website called "Finding Annie Schmidt." Interestingly, some people had become administrators on this site whom I didn't even know. People were posting all kinds of comments and suggestions. Most everything posted was kind and supportive, but it became apparent that it was unclear as to how the search effort should proceed. Some organizations instigated prayer vigils and the like from this site.

There was another site that had been created for those who were still actively physically searching the Columbia River Gorge. This site was mostly informative as to what areas were being searched, which days they had been searched, and by whom.

As I forced myself out of my personal fog, I was blown away at all of the efforts people were giving in our behalf. I was truly humbled. I asked myself, "How can people be so kind? How can so many be so invested on our behalf? I don't think that I'm half as good of a person as these people are. Would I do this same thing for someone else?" From all that I discovered about the efforts being made, I received such a witness of the goodness of others.

The fall Annie disappeared was an election year, and the political rhetoric was as volatile as I had ever seen in my lifetime. But I can testify that many, many people are good and kind. I wish so badly that our love for each other could be something that we would recognize and feel to an even greater degree. Because of the outpouring of support and love that we felt from so many, my love for others increased, regardless of any differences we may have.

For me and Jon, getting more of a handle on what was going on with search efforts only led to greater confusion and uncertainty as to what avenues we should pursue. This was way beyond our knowledge and ability to know what to do. We felt completely dependent upon the Lord to guide us. So I went to the Lord again, and in prayer I asked Him to guide us as we researched all these options.

"Heavenly Father, I do not know what to do. But I know You do. Please guide us, through the Holy Spirit, as I begin our research."

Then I spent a day contacting each person of significance on the websites. We spoke for hours to people and learned all that they knew. We found out what each person thought was the best course to take, what they planned to do, and what they had to offer. I can testify, as did Nephi, that "I was led by the Spirit, not knowing beforehand the things which I should do" (1 Nephi 4:6). As I spoke to individual after individual, the course we should follow slowly came into focus, like a camera lens being turned. We could feel which avenues were futile, and we could feel in which direction we should focus our efforts.

At the end of that day, I felt confident that the course we should pursue was to do another dog search. I had spent hours on the phone with a woman from Idaho named Annie Castiel. She had done search and rescue with dogs years ago in Colorado, before she lost her leg in an accident. Annie Castiel had been miraculously brought into the search for my Annie after learning about her disappearance through social media. When I spoke with her, I could tell that she was a voice of reason and had knowledge regarding dog search and rescue. She was willing to try to assemble dog teams to go back to Oregon and search again for our daughter. I felt very good about Annie Castiel, and I put her in touch with John Harding to coordinate our efforts.

Annie Castiel's willingness to become so heavily involved in organizing dog teams to search for my Annie reaffirmed my certainty that God had led me to trust her. And oh, how grateful I was and am for Annie's willingness to invest herself in this effort! How grateful I am for the precious gift of the Holy Ghost, who guided me to trust Annie Castiel when I was walking blindly in the dark trying to figure out how best to proceed in our search efforts.

For many reasons that we were unaware of as novices to search and rescue, Annie Castiel had a very daunting task in trying to assemble dog teams. Apparently there are a lot of political and ego issues that come into play, certain rules or protocols surrounding dog teams going into other dog teams' territories.

So, as Annie Castiel reached out to dog handlers in Utah and surrounding states, she was turned down again and again because they would each call up to the Oregon area and talk to the handlers who had already searched in the gorge for our daughter. These handlers would say, "We have already searched all over. There is no need to come and do it again." This meant that Annie Castiel received rejection after rejection from handlers who felt another search would be a waste of time.

Poor Annie was at the end of her rope when she called John Harding to tell him that she had been unable to find any teams willing to do the search. Again, the faith of John Harding came into play as he encouraged her by saying, "Now, Annie, that is not going to stop you from finding some dog teams that will accept our request, is it? I'm sure you will be able to find someone tomorrow."

In addition to John's encouragement, Annie Castiel had an experience that gave her the strength and faith to keep trying, especially when she felt defeated at being turned down by so many dog handlers who were unwilling to help in the search. She related the following:

"[One] night, I sat on my bed and I literally spoke to Annie. . . . I told her I was trying so hard and to please help me. I prayed to God. That night, I felt Annie's presence as I tried to sleep. I closed my eyes and I could see where she was and what the view was from where she was lying on the ground. She was in between two rock walls in a slide out or scree area, looking up at the night sky in a small clearing in the canopy. And she asked me not to quit. How could I?"

And so, Annie Castiel kept trying. And sure enough, she was eventually able to find some teams willing to go up and look again, despite all the discouragement they received from past teams. Again, this was miraculous.

In addition, there were two men in our area in Bountiful who had organized a bank account for people to donate to for the search. This was an enormous blessing for us because it ended up being the means to fund the final dog search. Again, we were so grateful for and overwhelmed at the goodness and kindness of these people. I actually never found out everyone who donated, but I thank you for your kindness. I'm just so grateful.

*Dave Forker and "Loki," Maire Ginman and "Guiness," Janice Holley and
"Scout," Joe Jennings and "Gunny," Paul Delong and "Taylor," John Harding,
Opie John and "Olaf," Annie Castiel, and Collette Daigle-Berg and "Chapter."*

Even though we were making plans to do another dog
search, there were still volunteers in Oregon who were searching every day. Each day I woke up hopeful that that day would
be the day that Annie was found.

After receiving the scrapbooks, I felt so profoundly that
Annie and Heavenly Father were reaching out to me and letting me know of their love, and that they were aware of my
hurt and struggle as a mother. This feeling that they were aware
of us and our struggle led me to feel that they would surely
help us find Annie. I had greater hope in my heart than I had
before I received the scrapbooks. It was my birthday week. It
would be the perfect time to find Annie. I thought, "Doesn't it
make sense that now would be the perfect time for our prayers
to be answered?" But, even as I thought this, the fact that several people who had gone missing in the Gorge were never
found weighed heavily on my mind.

Then, John Harding suggested we invite everyone who was invested in our struggle to unite with us in a fast on November 6, the first Sunday of the month. We would draw upon the faith of hundreds, maybe thousands, petitioning the Lord to answer our prayers and lead us to find Annie.

When John suggested this, I immediately knew in my heart that we wouldn't find Annie that week. We needed to do the fast. We needed to invite many to fast with us because Heavenly Father needed to use this experience to bless lives. People needed to fast, to exercise and grow their faith. As I realized this, a peace was given to my mind and heart that we needed to be patient and trust the Lord's timing. This experience was bigger than ourselves—we were being used as instruments in the Lord's hands for the blessing and strengthening of many lives. The Holy Ghost revealed to me that this was so, and I felt blessed and grateful to be a partner with the Lord in accomplishing His purposes. I felt peace that Annie wouldn't be found until after the fast.

We fasted on that Sunday and asked all involved to kneel with us in prayer at 5:00 p.m. and petition our Heavenly Father to please bless us to find our missing daughter. We asked that God would grant us the ability to feel peace and resolution through being able to find Annie's body and bring it home and lay it to rest. Jon and I especially felt the weight of thousands of people's faith in God on our behalf, and we so desired for that faith to be realized through answered prayers, especially for the children praying for us. I really wanted the children to know that Heavenly Father had heard and answered their prayers.

I was willing to accept if Heavenly Father had another plan

for this whole thing, but I asked Him, according to His omnipotent knowledge, that if it were expedient, He would please let all of these prayers be answered. Again, we were humbled and overwhelmed at the love and support we felt from so many. We were truly blessed beyond measure.

The dog searchers were scheduled to begin later that week, on November 10 and 11. John Harding and Annie Castiel were going up to organize and lead the search. Two of my brothers were also going back up to be a part of these final searches. In addition, there were many kind people who had continued to search on their own over the weeks since Annie's disappearance. One of them, Lydia McGranahan, was an avid hiker who had had some remarkable experiences that kept her committed to the search for Annie. Lydia was one of the people who kept going back to the gorge and searching on her own, day after day.

On the night of October 24, 2016, Lydia had a dream she was hiking the Munra trail. And then, in her dream, she was suddenly falling. As she fell, she felt like she was Annie. She woke abruptly before she landed and felt convinced that Annie was on Munra. The very next day, Jon discovered on Annie's computer a message between Annie and a friend saying they wanted to hike the Munra trail together. This added to Lydia's feelings that Annie was indeed on Munra.

On October 26, Lydia was back at base camp ready for a day of searching when John Harding mentioned to all gathered that they were open to any inspirations, dreams, or visions that anyone may have had regarding Annie's whereabouts. Lydia hesitantly shared with John her dream about Annie falling somewhere on Munra. Even though the Munra trails had been searched again and again, Lydia spent the day with her team bushwhacking and rappelling all over Munra, on and off trail. But still she was unsuccessful.

On October 29, Lydia went with another friend back to Munra and spent the day searching along the tops of the Munra cliffs, with yet another day of no results. And still, Lydia couldn't rest. She couldn't stop thinking of Annie and feeling that she was somewhere on Munra. Lydia went back on November 4 yet again. She described her experience with words like "slide, fall, pull, climb, scratches, bruises, search and search and search. But yet, another day with no Annie."

At this point, Lydia began to feel her strength and passion slipping. She had given so much and was so determined, but this search honestly felt like looking for a needle in a haystack.

As I've mentioned before, the terrain in the mountains along the Gorge is like nothing I've ever seen anywhere else. Though the trails are not bad, once you go off trail there are so many places where footing is unstable. Besides the green, wet, moss that makes everything so slippery, there is shale rock that is impossible to get a footing on, often forcing you to move on your hands and knees. Whichever direction you're determined to head, you might be thwarted by fallen trees and branches and slippery boulders. I had never seen anything like it, and with my back problems and my ankle that wouldn't bend, it was almost impossible for me to navigate on the off-trail mountainside.

The fact that Lydia was such a skilled hiker enabled her to do what I couldn't. She had already spent so many days searching, it was no wonder that her strength began to fail. She also had a daughter and husband whom she left at home each time she spent the day out on the mountain looking for my daughter, which must have added to Lydia's failing heart to continue the search for Annie.

But then, on Sunday, as she and her daughter were leaving their nondenominational Christian church meeting, her daughter said to her, "Mom, as we were singing in church, I felt like God was talking to me. And I know that you're going to find Annie."

"I'll find her?" Lydia said.

"You will," her daughter answered.

At that moment Lydia's strength was renewed, and she replied, "Oh, you know I will. I will."

On Thursday morning, November 10, 2016, eight dogs and their handlers from Utah, Wyoming, Montana, and Idaho gathered at base camp at the off-ramp of I-40 East, along with John Harding, Annie Castiel, my brothers, Lydia, and a few other friends and locals who, like Lydia, had never stopped their searching.

It was a beautiful, crisp fall morning. The weather was clear, which was unusual for that time of year. But that day was a perfect day for the search. As the searchers divvied up assignments, Lydia was assigned to Wauna Point. She immediately asked to be switched to Munra, so she was reassigned to search Munra with Joe Jennings, president of Great Basin K9 Search and Rescue, and his golden retriever dog, Gunny.

Lydia led them up the Munra switchback about six hundred feet, and then Joe let Gunny go, saying, "Adios," the command given to search for human remains. The going was slow, with thick vegetation, a lot of bushwhacking, and steep, difficult terrain to navigate.

Then it happened.

In Lydia's words: "Joe's dog popped up his head. I saw it immediately in Gunny, the attitude, nose up, whole body changed, faced uphill. Gunny had caught a scent."

They worked their way up under Munra cliff, but then Gunny seemed to lose the scent. Lydia described it this way, "The winds were swirling and Joe said that Gunny was trying to figure it out."

Eventually, with Gunny unable to pinpoint the scent, the team needed to head back down to the trailhead. Lydia remembers, "Joe's dog sat at the cliff's edge, head up, barking. Gunny was frustrated. He didn't want to go. He knew Annie was close."

Lydia headed down the mountain with Joe and Gunny and then went right back up again later that afternoon with a

Gunny alerting that he caught a scent.   *Lydia, Liz, and Reu, ready to search.*

dog named Olaf. He also caught a scent and began running up the hill into the thick underbrush. But again, the winds were swirling, and Olaf couldn't maintain the scent.

It was getting dark, and it was time to get off the mountain. They hadn't found Annie, but the fact that two dogs had marked a scent in the same area was a huge find. No other dogs on any of the other trails that day had had any success.

As they gathered at base camp at the end of the day, the consensus was that they would head home earlier Friday than previously anticipated. They reasoned that the area where the two dogs had marked was somewhere along the cliffs, and that at this point the search would involve technical climbing and helicopter.

Lydia, John Harding, Annie Castiel, and my brothers didn't want to end the search so soon. But after much discussion, they decided to just go out on Friday morning one more time before leaving later that day.

Lydia arrived early Friday morning along with a new handler, Liz Hall from Wyoming, and her young German shepherd dog, Reu. They actually hadn't planned to let Reu go out that day because he was so young and inexperienced, but Liz and Lydia both got there before anyone else, and so Lydia headed off with Liz and Reu back up the Munra trail.

Lydia took them right back to the spot where both Gunny and Olaf had marked the day before. Reu sniffed the air, immediately caught a scent, and took off up the hill. Liz couldn't keep up with Reu, but she called to Lydia to chase after her dog.

Reu continued to go higher and higher, heading east, right up to the base of the Munra cliffs. And then, as Lydia scrambled and crawled and ran to keep up, Reu stopped.

It was about 11:00 on Friday morning, November 11, 2016. I was just getting ready to go to the temple. Here I was, home in Utah, while there were people in Oregon at that moment looking for my daughter. I didn't know what else to do other than spend the day in the temple in fasting and prayer.

Just as I finished getting ready, I received a call from John Harding. Jon and Sarah were with me, and we put John on speaker.

"One of the dogs found the remains of someone, but we don't think they could be Annie because the remains are so decomposed."

My first thought was, "Oh, good! If the dogs were able to find this person, then they will be able to find Annie as well." I was so happy the searchers had found someone, and I was so happy for the family of whomever they had found.

Then John said, "There are several items along with the remains. Lydia has forwarded some pictures to me. Do you want me to forward them to you so you can see if you can identify anything?"

We emphatically answered, "Yes! Yes, of course!"

As the photos came in, John Harding was still on the phone with us. We looked at the pictures. I was shocked. I exclaimed, "That is her backpack! It's the one that Jonny used in high school and gave to her to use while he was on his mission. And that is her shoe! Those are her socks! Those are her books! John, this is Annie. All of these things are Annie's."

John Harding couldn't believe it because the remains were so decomposed. He said they would notify the authorities, and that there would have to be a positive identification done, probably through the teeth.

But for me, Jon, and Sarah, we were sure it was Annie. She had been found.

As we got off the phone, the three of us dropped to our knees in prayers of humble gratitude. As we prayed, I thought of when Alma and his people were delivered from bondage. "They poured out their thanks to God because he had been merciful unto them . . . and had delivered them . . . for they were in bondage, and none could deliver them except it were the Lord their God. And they gave thanks to God" (Mosiah 24:21–22). We prayed in gratitude that God had in part delivered us from bondage through the means, effort, and faith of so many good people, including John Harding, Annie Castiel, Lydia McGranahan, and all those involved in this last search.

Sometimes blessings are too great to even take in. Our finite minds and hearts and understandings are limited in grasping the magnitude of the events that happen to us. This is how we felt then. We couldn't even fully comprehend that we had been delivered, that we truly had found Annie. The magnitude of this blessing was so great that we had to let the reality of it slowly distill upon us over and over to an even greater degree. Even at this time, to this day, the whole experience feels so surreal. And yet, the kindness and deliverance of our great God continues to be a discovery to my mind and heart, filling me with so much humility and gratitude. He was so merciful and loving to let us find our daughter. The way it all came together was nothing short of a miracle, and we could see His hand orchestrating all things in His time, in His way, to fulfill His purposes.

The remains were positively identified as Annie. It was believed that she had gone bushwhacking right up to the base of the cliffs of Munra, attempted to climb—probably to get to

My brother, Jesse Anderegg, and friend,
Dave Perry, retracing Annie's climb.

a position to take a great picture—then slipped on the moss-covered rocks, falling somewhere between sixty to one hundred feet. It is my hope and belief that she died on impact.

In addition, Annie's phone was found among her other belongings. I am not sure why we were not able to get a correct ping on her phone from the beginning of the search. If we had, we might have found her within the first week of her disappearance. But, characteristically true to Annie, she had taken pictures and snaps along her hike that day.

My brother Jesse was able to get actual GPS coordinates off of each of Annie's pictures. He and his Oregon resident friend Dave Perry, who was one of the searchers who never stopped looking for Annie from the beginning, went back and retraced Annie's hike.

They found each of Annie's stops where she took pictures, which eventually led right to the base of the cliffs. Jesse and Dave then went to the top of the cliffs and rappelled down to see if there was any evidence of Annie's climb and fall. They found portions on the cliff's surface where moss had been scraped off, tree limbs broken off, and definite impressions in the ferns below. After Jesse's and Dave's additional investigations, we felt even more confident that Annie had slipped tragically and fallen.

I don't believe that Heavenly Father caused Annie to die, nor that her passing was necessarily His will. But I do believe that "all things work together for good to them that love God" (Romans 8:28), and that God is able to bless and guide His children in such a way that the most possible good can come of a tragedy such as this. And I can tell you that Annie would have been so on board with that. She was all about bringing souls to Christ. I can see her being so excited that she could be a part of the great good that came about through her death. I just know her, and I know this is how she feels.

My beautiful daughter had been found. Her phone and her driver's license were also found with her belongings. There was not much left of her physical body; she was positively identified by her teeth. I'm actually grateful we were able to find only her bones. It would have been really disturbing to find her body in any other way that actually resembled her. This also might have been a blessing in the Lord's timing.

Annie's spirit is whole, safe, and sound in the spirit world. And one day she will be resurrected in her perfect form. Every bit of her physical body will be restored to its proper frame— and so will mine. We will both be able to run and hike with awesome, strong, resurrected bodies. For this great gift, we give thanks to Jesus Christ. He is the firstfruits of them that sleep, the only one who could have brought about the Resurrection, through His infinite Atonement. Because of His sacrifice, we have a lot to look forward to. And I can't wait.

Conclusion: Love

I think the most important thing that I've learned through losing Annie is how I have been carried by the love of our Savior Jesus Christ, and because of this I've learned of our ever-present need to be filled with greater love for one another.

Matthew 22:36–40 says, "Master, which is the great commandment in the law? Jesus said unto him, Thou shalt love the Lord thy God with all thy heart, and with all thy soul, and with all thy mind. This is the first and great commandment. And the second is like unto it, Thou shalt love thy neighbour as thyself. On these two commandments hang all the law and the prophets."

I wouldn't say this is one of my greatest strengths. By nature, I'm instinctively selfish, self-consumed, and self-absorbed. I've spent the last twenty-six years trying to overcome these things and become a "new creature," and luckily, I've seen myself make progress. But I can just picture some people reading this book who knew me at different times in my life thinking, "Is this the same person I knew?" And I would have to answer, "No. I'm not the same person. Because of the Atonement of Jesus Christ, I'm not the same person."

Hopefully I'll continue to change more and more every day, and hopefully for the better. That is the goal, anyway. And one of the things that I want and need to become better at is loving unconditionally, empathetically, and unreservedly.

This was the spiritual gift that Annie possessed. Believe me, Annie was not perfect. She struggled with so many things, including personal insecurities and eating disorders. Her faith was even tested after her mission as she began to have a real wrestle with some of the cultural aspects of the Church. In so many ways she was an enigma to me. But because of Annie's gift of perfect love, her greatest goal in life was to reach out to those around her who she felt were suffering or just needed a friend.

Annie caught this vision in her ninth-grade year, and as she headed into high school she was determined to spend her years at Bountiful High reaching out and lifting those around her. In an effort to not be tied down to any one group, she kind of drew apart from the activities and friends she had associated with in junior high so that she would notice anyone who needed her and be a friend to all.

She would seek out those with whom she could spend a weekend night, always on the lookout for the lonely or downtrodden. She envisioned that her actions of befriending the friendless would catch on and spread, so that pretty soon everyone would accept and love and befriend everyone else, and

Jonny, Annie, Sarah, and Chris.

the school would become a huge, united school of friendship and love. That was her dream, anyway. And when she realized that one little girl didn't have the power to change everyone else and their perceptions of others, making her feel lonely in her mission to love perfectly, she would lose herself in service.

She did this in part by dedicating herself to helping and promoting her little brothers and sister and their friends in such a way that hopefully she could instill in them the dream she had of getting everyone to befriend and reach out to each other in unity. She was the most fun big sister anyone could have.

She drove her siblings and their friends all over the place so that they could have a good time. And the whole time, she tried to teach them to use their popularity or good fortune to reach out and befriend others.

When Annie graduated, the twins were just entering high school. She wrote them a long letter of advice that I later titled "Annie's Manifesto." She wrote:

Dear Jonny and Chris,

. . . If you want to truly be remembered and have a lasting influence and effect on your school and community, strive to always be motivated by love. Desire to serve because you care about your eternal brothers and sisters all around you (and not to mention potential eternal best friends). The best kind of leader is motivated by charity, the pure love of Christ. And something I know to be true is that charity never faileth!

In other words: if you sit by lonely people at lunch because you care about them, you will be happy. If you invite people who are different, the same, insecure, mediocre, stand out, or blend in, to join your friend circle (in class, at events, etc.), and if they can feel that care and charity from you, and see the effect of them grasping the fact that you are doing this, not for attention or to be popular or to be good or whatever, but for them, you will be happy.

If you ask a girl on a date who may not be the most popular or pretty, but who maybe had a wise and inspiring comment in seminary, and you want her to know that she is of great worth, and that you admire and encourage her strenuous efforts to do what is right, seeing and feeling the appreciation in her eyes and from her heart, will make you happy.

Take even just one song during each school dance to dance with someone who might be on the outskirts, and truly dance with them, get them to open up, do it for them. (Not to show them your best dance moves.) Have them show you their best moves. Compliment them. Build them up. If they are shy or nervous to start to dance then say, "Let's do it together!" They will feel cared for, special, important, and maybe even cool.

You will see those emotions in their eyes and feel it from their heart, and you will feel happy.

So, here's the thing, I could go on and on. But it would be so cool if you guys could take the idea of leading with charity and just make it your own! Keep the Spirit with you, and do any and every random thing He prompts you to do. And I promise that you will make a mark for good, not only in the heart of your school, but upon each and every human heart you take even just five minutes to care for and to encounter every day. I promise that this mark you make will be lasting.

Annie Schmidt

This Manifesto is the essence of who Annie was and is in a nutshell. This is what I'm striving to become more like. And, especially since losing Annie, I have felt that the Lord is trying to teach me to be like this and to love more deeply.

As I look around me and see all the different challenges people are struggling through—whether they be spiritual, physical, emotional, financial, mental, or social—I know that loving them the way Annie did, and the way Jesus does, will help carry and ease their burdens.

I know the way I can love everyone around me more per-fectly is to cling to the truths of the restored gospel of Jesus Christ, including clinging to the Book of Mormon, like my life depended on it, because it teaches and testifies so clearly of the divinity of Jesus Christ and the love He has for all of us. I can absolutely and without hesitation say that the Book of Mormon has been a major source of my strength to get through losing Annie. It has been a daily reminder to me that Christ is the rock and sure foundation upon which I can stand when I am faced with crushing experiences. And on days when

I stand confidently upon the rock of Christ and His love, or even on days when I feel like I'm barely holding on, I hope I can help others turn to Christ and His love for strength each day. If I can do this, hopefully I will be able to help others know how to weather the storms and even have joy. I hope I can help others to see the hand of the Lord sustaining them—and I hope they will be able to testify that it was the Savior who led them through. This deep personal testimony is what led me through, and is still leading me through, losing Annie.

As I seek to love as Annie did, I hope I can be a little more sympathetic and a little more empathetic toward others. I hope my challenges humble me and cause me to judge less and to love more. If I'm not sure how to navigate through some of the trials I experience, hopefully I won't turn around and criticize

Beautiful Annie.

someone else for how they are handling their own hardships. Hopefully I can be more compassionate. Hopefully I will reach out in love and support others. This is not to suggest that I won't stand for what I believe to be true and right. But, oh, I could go a long way at developing within myself the pure love of Christ. This was the gift Annie had, regardless of who or what the person was.

In an Instagram post made on September 18, 2016, Annie said, "Don't forget the happy thoughts. . . . All you need are happy thoughts." My happy thought is that Jesus Christ carries us through it all and loves us perfectly. My happy thought is that because of Jesus Christ we all will be resurrected and have the chance to be united. Because of Jesus Christ, through the Prophet Joseph Smith, the gospel of Jesus Christ, along with the priesthood authority to administer saving ordinances, has been restored to the earth in these latter days. Because of these ordinances and covenants, my family is sealed together for all time and throughout all eternity. And because of this sealing, Annie is bound to me forever and ever. In these truths reside my happy thoughts.

Thank you, Annie, for coming into this world and doing your best to make it a better place. You had a huge heart, and your life's work was to reach out to others and seek to help them to feel the love that the Savior has for them. You did such a good job! I'm so proud of you! Way to go, sweetheart! Thank you for letting me be your mother, to be molded by you and to have grown through our time together on this earth.

I look forward to the day when I can sit in a booth in the corner of an IHOP and bask in the shared love of our family as we did that day so many years ago. To me, IHOP will be heaven. I love you, Annie. Until we meet again.

PART 4
Tributes

Annie Schmidt
June 16, 2016

When people ask me why I do things I want to honestly be able to answer: because of love.

Twitter

Kanela Adamson:

"One day we were examining a poem about popularity and the teacher kept repeating the word 'popular' during the discussion.

"After the third or fourth time that word was thrown around, Annie raised her hand and, as if she couldn't hold it in any longer, burst out, 'Can we please stop using the word popular? I hate that word! What does that word actually mean anyway? We should just throw it away and everyone just be nice to each other.' She went on about how we all can make others feel 'popular,' and by doing so we can just forget about that word.

"That stuck with me for years after, because if everyone could love and be kind the way that Annie was to everyone she met, the world would be a brighter, happier, and safer place. . . .

" . . . Each time I meet new people, I think about what Annie said in that English class, and I try to treat them the way that Annie would."

Annie Schmidt
October 10, 2016

Why hold back the love?

Instagram

McKayla Knickrehm:

" . . . From the day I met Annie, I knew there was something special about her. She has a light that can't be missed. Her heart is as big as they come. At the time Annie and I met, I had to get surgery on both of my ankles, which made it so I was in a wheelchair. Annie took it upon herself to be my personal wheelchair pusher, and yes, she probably ran me into the wall at least two times a day. (Lol!) But, I knew without a doubt she was going to be standing outside of my class ready to push me to my next class.

"There was a time it was snowing, probably two feet of snow on the ground, but that didn't stop Annie. She pushed me all the way to the car and at one point tried to pick me and the wheelchair up at the same time all by herself. I believe it was Spencer who came to the rescue to help.

"Annie and I shared more than cheer together, we shared a friendship that changed my life. Whenever Annie would walk in a room she would hop in with the most welcoming smile and just say, 'Hey guys! What's up?'

"No matter what mood I was in, right at the moment I saw her smile, it would put a smile on my face also."

Marcus Lindmeir:

"The first time I met Annie was at BHS on a morning when we had a massive wind storm in Bountiful. As I walked into the school the power was out and there were only me and one other person there, that person happened to be Annie.

"We talked for a bit before deciding to head home, but then

Annie suddenly challenged me to a dance battle in the foyer of the school with all the lights out and the light beaming through the windows, because it made the perfect stage.

"And so, we dance battled! For hours. Then she suggested we run to her house to grab better speakers and invite more people to come and have a dance off at the school in the dark. Soon we had a good twenty people in the school having a dance off. That was the start of finding a real genuine beautiful relationship with Annie."

Emily Howe:

"Annie had a way of loving with her whole heart. She had a way of living life with passion. She showed me the importance of being a friend to everyone, because she was a friend to me. She was a friend in arguably the most crucial times in a girl's life. Being fourteen, fifteen, and sixteen is hard. You're trying to figure out who you are. You're awkward. Everyone else is awkward.

"But Annie wasn't. She treated me differently. She wasn't afraid to be my friend. In fact, she was excited to be my friend.

"Some of my favorite memories were on spring breaks in St. George. She more than happily dragged me around everywhere with her. She didn't care that I was a year younger or had really bushy hair and braces. She took me to all the high school parties.

"One night, after we got home from ice cream at Iceberg, we just sat looking at all the doors on the condos and talked for hours about how we wondered what was behind each door and the stories of the people inside. Annie was so curious about people and loved them for everything they were. She saw the best in people. She saw the best in me.

"Other memories include driving around with the windows down and music loud, just as she liked it. Looking back to a time that was one of the hardest and most crucial for who I am today, Annie is in my top ten most influential people. I'm who I am today because of Annie.

"Every day I'll strive to make others feel important and loved with my whole heart because of what Annie taught me. Annie teaches me to always, always, always, not just be a good friend, but a real friend. Annie inspires me to always dance to the music of life with joy, passion, and unconditional love."

Jessica Marie Winward:

"The last time I saw Annie I was visiting Portland, Oregon, with my family in August 2016. I don't remember why, but we were somehow unable to make it to the family church service, so we ended up awkwardly attending the Young Single Adult ward's fast and testimony meeting.

"Towards the end of the meeting, I saw a familiar face walk up to the pulpit—it was Annie. I smiled so big as I listened to her share her testimony of the Savior and the love that He has for every single person. Emotions that I had experienced as a fellow missionary in Georgia with Annie flooded me, and I felt sincere gratitude and joy.

"Annie hadn't lost any of her fire that she held as a sister missionary. I had no idea she had just moved to Oregon and she caught me up on all her latest adventures in being in several music bands.

"I was able to hug her before leaving, and she insisted on hugging everyone in my family as handshakes weren't 'her thing.' Ha, ha!"

Annie Schmidt
June 14, 2016

Let love in, in all its forms.

Twitter

Shannon Torres:

"Annie was so involved in everyone's life. She truly was a friend to everyone and made everyone feel loved. I remember in choir, I would always sit by Annie, and every day she made me feel like the most important person to her.

"She would always compliment me, and she made me feel loved in a world that was tough as a high school teenager. Annie is so inspiring and is a pure example of Christ-like love!"

Annie Schmidt
August 16, 2016
Feeling super thankful for all of the amazing friends and examples in my life. I hope to love others the way they have loved me.
Instagram

Emily Jarman:

"One of my favorite memories of Annie happened the beginning of our sophomore year. She and I sat next to each other in our computer tech class. On the first day of class she asked me if I had yet caught the 'Bieber fever.'

"Not yet knowing who Justin Bieber was, I was seriously confused.

"She then pulled out a notebook, binder, pencil, all with Justin Bieber on it. I was dumbfounded. She laughed, telling me how she was crazy about him.

"This new Bieber craze wasn't the only thing that surprised me during class with Annie.

"I hardly knew her, and yet, she talked to me with such genuine enthusiasm that any onlooker would've believed we were long time childhood best friends. I soon discovered that for Annie, this was not unusual. She was everyone's best friend, or at least treated them as such. I would call it a gift, one of her best qualities.

"I was among one of the lucky ones who was influenced by Annie's radiating light on an almost daily basis. She was consistently different from the rest of the crowd. Unafraid to be Annie. Unintentionally letting others know that it was safe to be themselves.

From temple Tuesdays, to late night restaurant trips, to lunches at her home, to after-dance activities at her house. I'm truly a better person for having known Annie."

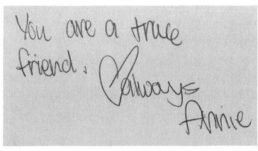

A note from Annie.

Megan Davis Smith:

"Annie means power and confidence, unconditional love and Christ-like acts. She was the first person to include me in anything. She was bold enough to tell me to stop conforming and be myself. We had so many adventures that made me laugh till I cried. Annie means fun, good times, good experimental music, and food.

"Along with the fun and hilarious times there were countless extremely spiritual times. I cried often, talking to Annie on hikes, where we would talk about the Church and our testimonies and how much we loved each other.

"All in all, I would say that of all the people that have been influential in my life, Annie is among the top five. I'm eternally grateful for her."

Jessica Sullivan:

"These are words Annie wrote to me in a note, 'Alone we may feel like we make a very small difference, but with Him, we can do all things, especially as a whole, unified.'"

Maddi Dunn Richardson:

" . . . I often noticed that Annie would talk to everyone, and quickly realized that she truly saw all people as equals. She didn't speak to others out of obligation, and she wasn't just trying to be nice. I could tell she really cared about people.

"During our senior year we had choir together. On one of the nights of our concert, I remember I was having a rough day and keeping to myself a little more than usual. Annie came over and struck up a conversation with me like I was one of her good friends. That's just not something that usually happens in high school, even with the nicest of people. She was genuinely kind to me, and we talked and laughed for quite a while.

"I don't know if she realized what that meant to me, but it made the entire evening easier, and seriously made me think about what I could do to be a better friend. I can only imagine how many lives Annie has touched, and feel fortunate that I went to school with her."

Abigail Moon:

"One of my favorite memories with Annie was one day during lunch break. We went to her house and made bagels, then sat on her roof and ate them, while we talked and laughed. It was the happiest!

"Those many, many conversations were all wonderful and I loved them, but I think about Annie, and I realize that what impacted me most were not the words she spoke, but definitely the way she made me feel. I'll never forget it. Ever. I don't think anyone ever will.

"People always felt special around her. Noticed. Loved. Important. She has a God-given gift of limitless heart. I don't think she could ever run out of room to love. Annie came and changed the world."

Annie sharing her love with a stranger.

Lindsey Parrish:

"Annie randomly came to midnight sushi with a group of friends one summer night in 2011. As we exited the restaurant there was a homeless woman playing the guitar. We all hurried past, but Annie stopped, knelt down in front of this woman, and folded a dollar bill into a ring.

"She told the woman how beautiful her music was, and put the dollar bill on her finger, while we all stood a safe distance away watching.

"This stuck with me for years. Annie was always so kind to everyone."

Elena Mederios:

"Annie was the most spontaneous and loving girl I have ever met. At the end of 6th grade she threw a party at her house. In my mind, Annie was one of the 'cool' girls, but she definitely didn't act that way.

"I remember I was sitting out on the playground after school and noticed she was handing out envelopes to all her friends. I was curious to what was inside and soon realized it was for a party, as everyone began talking about it.

"I kept reminding myself that Annie really didn't have any idea who I was, but oh how dearly I wished I were cool enough to be invited to this party.

"As I sat on the cement waiting for my mom to pick me up after school, I soon noticed someone walking towards me. I looked up to find Annie's big smile and an envelope in her hand.

"'Hey Elena, I'm not sure what you're doing Friday night, but here's an invitation to my party. You should come!'

"I was stunned and at a loss for words. Couldn't believe it. She even wrote my name on the envelope. I literally couldn't stop smiling the rest of the day.

"Fast forward to Friday night, I was extremely nervous to go to the party because I was just the nerdy soccer girl. I had never associated with all these cool kids before, but I figured I would go for a little. I remember walking in, feeling overwhelmed with the amount of unfamiliar and 'cool' faces I saw.

"However, I instantly made eye contact with Annie, and she came running over to me.

"'I'm SO glad you came! Here, come get some food with me.'

"Immediately I felt like a million dollars. 'Wow,' I thought. 'This girl really doesn't know me, but she treats me like I'm her best friend.'

"From that day on my love and appreciation grew tremendously for Annie. She always noticed the one and made them feel confident.

"Our paths didn't cross again until high school, specifically our senior year. Little did I know that girl from elementary would become one of my best friends. We both made Senior Class office and worked very closely together. She always had the most random and fun ideas for activities. She had an idea to write everyone in our senior class a note by the end of the year. She was very passionate about this and wrote many each week.

"I always found her eating lunch with the lonely one, starting a dance circle at school dances, and promoting school spirit at games with face paint and cheering her heart out. She was truly the life of the party in high school. Annie was one of the big reasons our senior class was so close knit. Everyone felt like they belonged. #WeAreOne

"Annie taught me to love more, adventure more, and be myself more. She truly emulates Christ and His love for others. So many people can attest that no one makes you feel more loved than Annie.

"Annie, I love you. I love your spunk, contagious smile, and craziness. Thank you for changing my life in ways I cannot even describe."

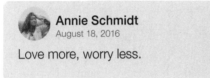

Annie Schmidt
August 18, 2016

Love more, worry less.

Instagram

Bailey Wood Knudsen:

" . . . On my very first day of high school as a sophomore, I was terrified for the future ahead of me. I was awkward, nervous, and desperate to fit in my new environment.

"Annie, a fun and outgoing student body officer, invited me and a few other sophomore girls out to lunch. In the car we all sang along to loud music and had so much fun. I had the best time and completely forgot about all of my nerves. I was instantly reassured that I would be just fine in high school because there were people like Annie. I made it a goal to make everyone feel as special as Annie made me feel.

"Although it was a small and seemingly insignificant gesture to ask a little sophomore girl to lunch, something she probably wouldn't even remember, Annie made a great impact on me. I'll always be thankful for her!"

Aubree Monson Weiler:

"There was never such a thing as an 'ordinary day' for Annie. Every day was another chance to listen to good music, go on an adventure, or find someone around her to help. She was always wanting and willing to make friends wherever she went, regardless of their circumstances, age, religion, or popularity factor. She didn't care, she saw the good in absolutely everyone.

"I'll never forget one specific day in choir. We all came to class and sat in our seats, and to our great surprise we found handwritten notes with a special treat on our seats. They were from an 'anonymous friend,' but I knew exactly who it was. It was Annie, because that is exactly the type of person she was. (Plus, I saw them in her backpack. Ha, ha)."

Emily Jensen:

"I danced with Annie for two years. During the time I knew her she was never short on energy, inspiration, and love. She danced everywhere, in the car, in the store, in her house, and was really the first person to teach me that being yourself is cool.

"She didn't fit her personality into a box, but had an endless range of emotions and feelings and experiences that couldn't be contained, and she didn't try to, especially when it came to her testimony.

"She shared her love for Jesus Christ and Heavenly Father at every possible moment. And she lived her life as a testament that loving the Lord isn't a sacrifice, but a blessing on those who love Him and love others like He does.

"One time we had a sleepover at her house, and we had a great time, but before we went to bed, she invited us to do a scripture study together. We all shared our favorite scriptures and the stories behind them, and the Spirit was so strong.

"Annie shared Moses 1:35, 'But only an account of this earth, and the inhabitants thereof, give I unto you. For behold, there are many worlds that have passed away by the word of my power. And there are many that now stand, and innumerable are they unto man; but all things are numbered unto me, for they are mine and I know them.'

"She talked about how when we feel like 'scum' we need to remember our divine and individual worth.

"She was so kind and friendly and open to everyone and always reserved time for people who needed her attention. She took time to talk to me and made me feel important at a time when I didn't feel like I was. I know she went through difficult times in her life, but her courage and her ability to enjoy life despite her sadness has been such an inspiration to me as I've struggled in my life.

"I found an Instagram post from her last year she'd put up of Christ staring at the stars with her caption, 'Can't wait to stargaze with my best friend.'"

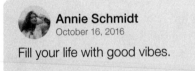

Annie Schmidt
October 16, 2016

Fill your life with good vibes.

Twitter

Explanation of Terms

Covenant: A sacred agreement between God and a person or group of people.

EFY: Especially for Youth, a week-long, youth-oriented seminar focused on fellowship and teaching the principles of The Church of Jesus Christ of Latter-day Saints.

Ensign: An official, monthly periodical of The Church of Jesus Christ of Latter-day Saints.

General Authorities: Men who are called to serve as special witnesses of Christ, to proclaim the gospel of Jesus Christ, and to build up the Church throughout the world.

Mission: A unit of the Church that normally covers an area much larger than that covered by a stake. Each mission is presided over by a mission president, assisted by two counselors. Mission presidents are directly accountable to General Authorities. Full-time missionaries serve for a period of eighteen to twenty-four months in a particular mission, serving and teaching anyone who will listen about the gospel of Jesus Christ.

Ordinance: A sacred, formal act performed by the authority of the priesthood. Some ordinances are essential to our exaltation and are called saving ordinances. With these saving ordinances, we enter into solemn covenants with the Lord.

Patriarch: One who is ordained to give special patriarchal blessings to members of the Church.

President of The Church of Jesus Christ of Latter-day Saints: A prophet, seer, and revelator whom the Lord calls to guide His covenant people. The President of the Church presides over the entire Church.

Priesthood: The word *priesthood* has two meanings. First, priesthood is the power and authority of God. It has always existed and will continue to exist without end. Through the priesthood, God created and governs the heavens and the earth. Through this power, He exalts His obedient children, bringing to pass "the immortality and eternal life of man" (Moses 1:39). Second, in mortality, priesthood is the power and authority of God that God gives to man to act in all things necessary for the salvation of God's children. The blessings of the priesthood are available to all who receive the gospel.

Quorum of the Twelve Apostles: Twelve men whom we sustain as prophets, seers, and revelators and who are "special witnesses of the name of Christ in all the world" (Doctrine and Covenants 107:23).

Relief Society: The women's organization in The Church of Jesus Christ of Latter-day Saints, founded by the Prophet Joseph Smith in 1842. The Relief Society's purpose is to increase faith in Heavenly Father and Jesus Christ and His Atonement, to strengthen individuals, families, and homes through ordinances and covenants, and to work in unity to help those in need.

Stake: A unit of the Church covering a specific geographical area. The term *stake* comes from the prophet Isaiah, who prophesied that the latter-day Church would be like a tent, held secure by stakes (see Isaiah 33:20; 54:2). There are usually five to twelve wards and branches in a stake. Each stake is presided over by a stake president, assisted by two counselors.

Tracting: The process by which full-time missionaries of The Church of Jesus Christ of Latter-day Saints find people to teach about the restored gospel of Jesus Christ. Tracting includes knocking door-to-door and contacting people on the street, bus, or any other social setting where missionaries might come in contact with people.

Veil: In this book, the word *veil* signifies the separation between this earth life and the spirit world or God's realm, or the separation between us and those who have passed.

Ward: A congregation of members of The Church of Jesus Christ of Latter-day Saints.

About the Authors

Michelle Schmidt is the mother of Annie Schmidt, who passed away in a hiking accident in Oregon in the fall of 2016. Michelle is married to Jon Schmidt of The Piano Guys. Michelle is also the mother of four other children. As a full-time stay-at-home mother, Michelle has dedicated her life to the raising of her five children and the care of many extended family members. Michelle earned a bachelor's degree in English from the University of Utah and enjoys reading, biking, dark chocolate, and big sycamore trees. Her favorite pastime is spending time with her husband and kids.

Angie Taylor is sister to Michelle Schmidt and aunt to Annie Schmidt. Angie is married to Brock Taylor, and is the mother of four children. Angie has an English degree with an emphasis in Creative Writing from New Mexico State University, is an author of both fiction and nonfiction, including *Twists in Time*, a young adult science fiction story, as well as a number of literary poems. *Carried* is her first co-written nonfiction piece as well as being one of the most sacred and special writing experiences she has had. If you'd like to learn more about Angie and her writing, visit angietaylorwrites.com.